Hanged by a Dream?

Hanged by a Dream?

The Facts Behind the Legend

Perry Deane Young

iUniverse, Inc.
New York Lincoln Shanghai

Hanged by a Dream?
The Facts Behind the Legend

Copyright © 2005 by Perry Deane Young

iUniverse books may be ordered through booksellers or by contacting:

iUniverse
2021 Pine Lake Road, Suite 100
Lincoln, NE 68512
www.iuniverse.com
1-800-Authors (1-800-288-4677)

ISBN-13: 978-0-595-36294-3 (pbk)
ISBN-13: 978-0-595-80734-5 (ebk)
ISBN-10: 0-595-36294-X (pbk)
ISBN-10: 0-595-80734-8 (ebk)

Printed in the United States of America

Contents

Introduction vii

Chronology xi

I.   The Legends 1

II. Searching for the Facts 4

III. Illustrations 33

    a. Execution order for Effler to be hanged. 33

    b. Portrait of Steve and Peggy Effler's son, Alfred Erwin Effler,
        and his wife, Maebelle Hughes Effler. 34

    c. Family of Steve Effler's half-brother, Joseph Effler;
        Francis Govan and Katherine Effler Lanning. 35

    d. Joshua Young's testimony; tombstone erected over
        Effler's grave by his descendants. 36

    e. First page of Effler's confession. 37

    f. Last page of Effler's confession. 38

IV. Five Versions of the Story 39

    a. From The Young Family, 1959...39

    b. From Aunt Zona's Web 41

    c. Mrs. Glenn's Account..45

    d. From Tar Heel Ghosts 50

    e. Monroe Thomas' Article 54

V.   Documents 74

VI. Descendants of Stephen and Margaret Effler 105

The Untold Story of Frankie Silver 137

About the Author 139

Introduction

There was a time when folks in what Thomas Wolfe called the "hill-bound, world-lost" reaches of the Appalachian mountains had plenty of time to meditate upon the past. After a hard day's work in the kitchen or the fields, they would sit and rock on the open porch and softly recall something hilarious Momma or Daddy had told them years and years ago. The howling winds and bitter cold in the harsh winters would remind them of the tales of horror that had been passed down for generations.

The old folks would stare into the fire and recollect this was how it must have happened because that was the way folks always said it happened. Frankie Silver had taken an axe and killed her husband and then chopped up the body—her family had to have helped her—and burned it in the fireplace. Young Steve Effler brutally beat his wife to death, choked her and broke her neck and almost got away with it—if old Josh Young hadn't had that dream.

Joshua Young was my grandfather's first cousin. I was born in 1941, about the time when world events and radio and television had just begun to invade even the most remote areas of Appalachia. Lucky for me, the hours of story-telling on the porch or before the fire hadn't yet been overwhelmed by the mass media. I grew up hearing bits and pieces of the tale about how Josh Young's dream had brought Steve Effler to justice and caused him to be hanged by the neck until dead. I started writing about the two murder stories—Frankie Silver and Steve Effler—when I was in high school in the 1950s. Like many hundreds of others before me, I repeated the stories as they had been passed down to me and as they had been published in countless newspaper and magazine articles. At first, it never occurred to me to question the details or look for facts behind the legends. But it eventually dawned on me that these were not tall tales about some fictional characters, these were real tragedies about living breathing human beings. And maybe, just maybe, the facts were far more complicated than the simple stories handed down from generation to generation.

Hanged by a Dream?

When I was a student at the University of North Carolina, in 1963, I discovered a set of documents relating to the Silver case in the governors' papers in the North Carolina Archives in Raleigh. The facts set forth in 17 letters and petitions told a radically different story of Frankie than the one handed down about the jealous fiend who sneaked up on her husband as he lay sleeping with his baby girl in his arms beside the fire. Aside from the name "Frankie" and that it was a woman who killed her man, the story had nothing whatever to do with the "Frankie and Johnny" ballad from the Mississippi delta. But the popularity of that song had over the years overtaken the facts about the tawdry truth of the Frankie Silver case. Frankie's husband, Charles Silver, was a hard-drinking, "lazy, trifling man" who abused his wife. She had killed him in self defense, but because of the laws of that time, she could not take the stand in her own defense and explain what really happened. At the height of the Watergate hearings in September of 1973, the late Sen. Sam Ervin—who was born just a few blocks from where Frankie was hanged in Morganton—took time out to write me a detailed letter saying he agreed with me that she was unjustly hanged. That's what the clerk of court told his daddy and his daddy told him.

After many years wandering about the globe as a journalist, from New York to Saigon to Beirut and Washington and San Diego, I finally came home to North Carolina in 1990. And, of course, all those wonderful stories passed down from my family were still embedded deep in my memory. I kept reading newspaper accounts—and one popular novel—about the Frankie Silver case that were full of mistakes and just plain wrong in their depiction of that poor woman. And, so, in 1998, I wrote my own account of the story, "The Untold Story of Frankie Silver, Was She Unjustly Hanged?" Under the old Southern storyteller's maxim, "Tell a Lie when the Truth Would Do," I published all the many tall tales and embellishments that had been added to the bare facts of the Frankie Silver case over the years. I also copied the extraordinary number of newspaper accounts, court documents, letters and petitions which contradicted nearly every one of those tales. After reading these, I think the reader will conclude as Sen. Sam Ervin and I did that history has done a disservice to this poor woman who only did what any sane person would do when her husband tried to kill her.

After gathering all the documents about that 1831 murder, it occurred to me that the Steve Effler murder case took place 50 years after that one. There must surely be even better records in the archives about that case. I went to the

North Carolina Archives Annex for the Supreme Court and to my delight, found 114 pages of documents relating to State v. Effler. I also began an extensive correspondence with the relatives and direct descendants of Effler and his murdered wife. This led me to the most chilling document I have ever run across in many years hearing the old tales and searching for the facts behind the stories. This was Effler's confession of the gory details of his crime.

There are many similarities between the Silver and Effler cases. Both involved very young couples in isolated cabins in the thick forests on the steep mountains of the Toe River valley that meanders through Yancey and Mitchell counties to the Tennessee line where the river becomes the Nolichucky River. In both cases, there was a tiny baby orphaned by the murder of one parent, the hanging of the other. But there are also many differences—most notably, Frankie was hanged because she was not allowed to take the stand in her own defense and tell the truth. Steve Effler was convicted at least in part because he did take the stand and lied. Unlike Frankie's confession, which turned public sentiment in her favor and caused hundreds of people to sign petitions to save her, Effler's confession convinced people he should have been hanged.

I have structured this book in what I hope is the most logical and readable sequence. In Part One, I begin with a composite of all the various legends that have grown up around the tale of Joshua Young's dream and Steve Effler's hanging. In Part Two, I describe my own search for the facts. Did Young actually have such a dream? Was it the key factor in stopping Effler and getting him tried for murder? What was the evidence presented at the trial? In Part Three, some Effler family photographs and other documents are reproduced to add some human faces to these stories. In Part Four, five different versions of the legend are reproduced as they have been handed down. In Part Five, all of the legal documents associated with the case are reproduced so the reader can draw his or her own conclusions.

And, finally, in Part Six, the book concludes on a note of hope with the family history of Stephen and Margaret Grindstaff Effler's son, Alfred Erwin Effler. Out of this hideous crime, an innocent babe grew up to be a man of substance and character who restored some dignity to the family name. His descendants now number in the hundreds.

Perry Deane Young
Chapel Hill, North Carolina

Chronology

-- February 4, 1860, Steven or Stephen Effler was born near Flag Pond, Tennessee.

-- 1860, Margaret "Peggy" Grindstaff was born at Red Hill in what was then Yancey, but is now Mitchell County, North Carolina.

-- March 30, 1879, Stephen Effler and Peggy Grindstaff were married in Yancey County, North Carolina.

-- Joseph W. Effler was born April 28, 1880 to Steve and Peggy Effler. His name was soon changed to Alfred Erwin Effler.

-- January 6, 1881, a Thursday, Steve Effler murdered his wife, but claimed to his family and neighbors she died while having a fit or seizure.

-- January 9, 1881, Sunday, the funeral procession was stopped on its way from Buck Creek Gap to the Grindstaff family cemetery in Red Hill.

-- January 10, 1881, a warrant for the arrest of Steven Effler was signed by Justice of the Peace W.F. Craig.

-- January 12, 1881, the warrant for murder was served and Steve Effler was committed to the McDowell County jail at Marion to await trial in the spring term of Superior Court.

-- March 28, 1881, spring term, Superior Court, a grand jury indicted Stephen Effler for murder and trial was scheduled.

-- March 30, 1881, Effler and his lawyer, James Madison Gudger, were granted a postponement of the case to fall term because they had not had time to prepare their case.

-- September 29, 1881, a special venire of 110 potential jurors was summoned.

-- October—, 1881, Stephen Effler was convicted of murder and Judge Augustus Seymour ordered the execution "on Friday the 11th day of November, 1881, on which day between the hours of eleven and two o'clock he shall be taken to the place of execution appointed by law and there be hanged by the neck until he be dead."

-- October 5, 1881, Effler appealed his conviction to the North Carolina Supreme Court.

-- October, fall term, 1881, Writing for the majority, Justice Thomas Ruffin affirmed the lower court decision and Effler's sentence of death was ordered to be carried out.

-- ????? Through his lawyer, Effler pleaded that he has "become insane since his trial and conviction." A court hearing determined he was not insane.

-- May 18, 1882, with his lawyer's help, Stephen Effler wrote a full confession.

-- May 19, 1882, Stephen Effler was hanged at Marion, North Carolina

I. The Legends

The way folks always said it happened was this: It was in the dead of winter; snow lay on the ground. Josh Young had just crawled into bed.

Some folks say he was asleep, but Josh always said he wasn't asleep. He was just laying there, about to doze off, when he saw this woman at the foot his bed.

She was a pretty young woman he had never seen before. She seemed to be pleading for help, but she didn't say anything. Her head was rolling about as if her neck was broken.

Josh woke up his wife and told her what he'd seen. "Aw, Josh, yer jist a dreamin'," she said. "Go back to sleep."

He tried, but every time he'd be close to sleep, there she'd appear again, pleading for him to help her. Finally, Josh gave up ever going to sleep. He got up, stoked the fire and sat there looking into the blaze, wondering what in the world to do about the vision he'd just seen.

The Youngs lived down on Brown's Creek. Along about daylight, Josh took off up the wagon road alongside South Toe River. He had to tell somebody; he had to do something. He stopped at Joe Murphy's and he'd just finished building a casket.

Josh asked him who had died, he hadn't heard about anybody dying in the neighborhood. "Yep," Murphy replied, it was Steve Effler's wife, young Peggy, who'd died the night before. "They're gonna bury her today I reckon."

"She didn't die," Josh suddenly declared, "she was murdered." "Why, Josh," Murphy said, "You better hush. Them Efflers'll kill you for talking like that."

But, Joshua Young was determined. He went on up to his friend Sandy Patton's house and told him about the vision he'd had and about the death of Peggy Effler. "Sandy," Josh said, "I declare she must have been the woman I saw. And if she was, she had a broken neck. She was murdered." Patton, too, told him he better watch his mouth, talking that way about one of the Efflers.

Patton knew the young couple, they lived in a little cabin just over Buck Creek Gap in McDowell County, not far from Effler's granddaddy's house on the Yancey side of the Blue Ridge.

Sandy Patton lived by the side of the road coming down from the gap and it wasn't long before they saw the little group of mourners coming along, carrying the casket on their shoulders. They stopped for a rest and Patton and Young went over to inquire about the deceased. They told him about how Peggy Effler had always suffered from asthma. She had come down with some sort of convulsions and died with her little baby in her arms. Steve, they said, had run for help to his grandfather's and other neighbors but by the time they all got back, the poor woman was already dead and there was nothing anybody could do but mourn. They said they were taking her body back to the burying ground of her people, the Grindstaffs, over toward Red Hill.

Pretending they just wanted to pay their respects, the two men had the casket opened and Josh Young stepped back with a gasp: this was the woman he'd seen in his dream or vision or whatever it was. As a Justice of the Peace, Young told the group he was ordering the body held until a doctor could come from Burnsville and examine her.

Well, they say the doctor was scared out of his wits when he saw how worked up everybody was. Steve Effler was carrying on, fit to be tied, one minute grieving about his wife, the next about the injustice of not being able to bury her. The Yancey doctor took one quick look at the corpse and declared she'd died of natural causes. He wanted nothing more to do with it all.

Once again, Joshua Young stood up and asserted his authority as magistrate for that whole area. He said he was going to send for the coroner in McDowell County, because that's where the crime was committed. It took several hours, a night and part of the next day, but Dr. Virgil Butts, a young man just starting his practice, finally came.

By this time, a room had been cleared out in Patton's house and the body was laid out on a table where it could be properly examined. Dr. Butts carefully examined the bruises around the poor woman's neck. He lifted her up and her head fell back. He said there was no question about it; this woman had been murdered. She had been badly beaten and her neck was broken.

There was a good sized crowd gathered up by then and some folks were rumbling about they oughta just hang Steve Effler right then and there. But the calmer heads prevailed and the sheriff was called. While they were waiting, Effler confessed and said he and his wife had argued—some said cause she'd burned the bread for supper that night—and he struck her and knocked her down. He picked up a piece of cloth and was trying to strangle her, but he was so strong he broke her neck instead.

Blood was all over the place but Effler cleaned up his wife's corpse and quickly turned over the floor boards. When the Sheriff and his men examined the cabin, they could see the boards didn't match; and underneath, they found the blood stains Effler had tried to hide.

Once he'd confessed, folks told it that an eerie calm seemed to come over Steve Effler as if he were possessed somehow. Outside the house that night, some swore they could see the devil—big as a mule and black as midnight—hovering ten feet above the ground. But, next morning, there were no tracks in the snow. The sheriff took Steve Effler south over the mountain to the jail in Marion and the family took Peggy's casket in the other direction north on over to Red Hill to be buried.

It didn't take the jury long to decide Effler was guilty and he was sentenced to be hanged. Folks said it was a clear day in the middle of June when Effler was hanged, but a storm came up and snow fell on the higher mountains.

Now, when they hang a person it's supposed to break their neck real quick like, so they don't just dangle there and suffer. However, folks said when they took Steve Effler's body down, they could tell the rope hadn't broken his neck, he'd strangled to death—the way he tried to kill his wife. If he hadn't broken her neck, nobody could ever have proved he killed her.

II. Searching for the Facts

The Setting

To drive through the area described in this book nowadays, you would think how lucky were these people to live in such an incredibly beautiful setting. In fact, today's paved Highway 80 follows much the same route over Buck Creek Gap across the Blue Ridge and down into the lush Toe River Valley as it did when this story took place more than 120 years ago. Like so many other roads, this one no doubt followed an old trail pounded out by herds of buffalo, America's original trailblazers and roadbuilders. Before being driven further and further west, those powerful native American animals roamed from coast to coast in herds numbering in the hundreds of thousands. The herds were extraordinary engineers because they had the innate sense to follow the paths of least resistance along the natural contours of the land. These paths became the hunting trails of the Indians and then the wagon roads of the European settlers and eventually the paved roads of modern tourists.

At the top of the Blue Ridge, the north-south Highway 80 is intersected by the Blue Ridge Parkway going east and west. This intersection at Buck Creek Gap is marked by one of the parkway's beautiful arched stone bridges. It is just steps away from the site of our gruesome tale on the McDowell side of the line between Yancey and McDowell counties.

Rising to the west is Mount Mitchell, highest mountain in eastern America, centerpiece of what the old folks called "the Black Mountain," because this whole range of peaks, well over 6,000 feet, were once impenetrable with a jungle growth of laurel and ivy, and nearly black with the dark green foliage of the balsam or Frasier fir trees that grow only at such an altitude.

You'd be right about the paradise-like setting as far as contemporary folks go. The steep mountainsides once useless for crops or grazing or anything else are now prime resort real estate, with fabulous views of the snow covered mountains in winter, the lush green of spring and summer and the magnificent red and yellow colors of fall.

But you'd be dead wrong about the setting at the time Steve Effler and his young wife, Peggy, settled into a little log cabin in December of 1880 just over the south side of Buck Creek Gap. Life was especially hard in this area in those days. The mountain people had suffered and suffered horribly from the devastation caused by the Civil War even though they were many miles from any major battles. Caught in between the Union troops in East Tennessee and the Confederates in North Carolina, they were subjected to constant foraging raids. Adding insult to injury were the local marauders with no politics whatsoever who just roamed about pillaging the hapless people and grabbing every last slab of bacon they could steal. "Don't matter who wins this war," said one old fellow in Yancey, "the people are going to lose."

It was a hardscrabble life at best, trying to scrape a living out of the rugged hillsides, just keeping body and soul together. It was a drab dull hard daily grind merely to keep clothes on the back and food in the belly. On top of that was the constant plague of diseases. If a woman managed to survive childbirth, she had the likelihood of seeing her babies die before they ever reached maturity. "The fevers" were rampant and deadly. Somebody in the household was sick with malaria or typhoid or scarlet or rheumatic fever near-about all the time.

Tensions ran deep among the young couples trying to start a new life, alone in isolated cabins in the wilderness. They knew nothing of modern terms like "manic depression" and had no means of treatment even if they had known a name for the debilitating life-weary lonesome blues that affected so many of them. There was no relief at all from the backbreaking hard work required to provide even the bare basics of human existence. Cabin fever was a bitter fact of life. We know of two young couples in the Toe River Valley of the 19th Century who turned on each other, Charlie and Frankie Silver and Steve and Peggy Effler. But, who knows how many others grew so restive and frustrated with each other they resorted to murder and nobody ever found out? Steve Effler came very close to getting away with the brutal murder of his wife. Like Frankie Silver, he was brought to justice by neighbors who stood up for what was right. Unlike Frankie, however, nobody ever felt Steve Effler's crime was justified. Several hundred people signed petitions to pardon Frankie Silver and save her from the gallows; nobody ever asked the governor to pardon Steve Effler. Everybody agreed he should have been hanged.

The Efflers

The bare fact of Steve Effler's birth is recorded in a Bible handed down to Hazel Hollingworth in Spruce Pine, North Carolina, from her great grandfather, Ira James Ratliff. The inscription does not tell us who his mother was and certainly not who his father was. It just says, "Steven Effler was born Feb. the 4 A.D. 1860." The name is spelled "Stephen" in all other records. We learn from family sources that Steve was born near what is now Morristown, Tennessee. His mother was Mary "Polly" Effler, who was born in 1841, the daughter of Henry and Margaret "Peggy" Grindstaff Effler. Nobody seems to know who Steve Effler's father was.

The old Bible recorded the birth of one other son Polly Effler had out of wedlock: "Joseph M. Effler was born July 24, A.D., 1870." A Yancey County Bastardy bond dated March 11, 1870 apparently refers to the second son and says that Steven McFalls was the father and also notes "conception on November 25, 1869," which would allow nine months for Joseph's birth the following July. A third birth is also recorded in the Bible: "Jobe P. Caraway was born March the 26 A.D. 1885." He was apparently the child of Polly's marriage on March 19, 1882 to David McClinton Caraway. Clint Caraway listed his age as 50 on the marriage certificate and gave no name for a father, but said his mother's name was Elizabeth Caraway and she was dead.

In spite of the rough circumstances of her existence, Polly Effler was a woman widely respected among her neighbors. In her account of the murder, Sallie Glenn says that her grandfather, David Byrd, born in 1815, always spoke highly of the hanged man's mother. She wrote: "Polly Effler was a good woman. In the days when they had their fields all fenced with rails and cattle and hogs ran at large, they had a forest fire and it looked like all they had would be burnt. Men and women were working to get the fire checked. Grandfather said he came on top of a ridge and there was Polly on her knees, hands reaching toward heaven, and crying to the Lord to send rain. He said it was not hours, it was then, while she was yet on her knees, that the rain came and he never saw in his life more rain. It poured and put out all the fire."

Polly Effler's father, Henry, was born about 1819 in North Carolina. Her grandfather, Lawrence or Lorance Effler, was born in Prussia in 1787 and died April 6, 1886 in Unicoi County, Tennessee. Descendants say his father, Michael, died and young Lawrence came from the old country with his widowed mother, Honor Effler, who later married John Chapple in Norfolk County, Virginia. Lawrence Effler volunteered in Captain Jesse Cole's Company, Wares Regiment, General Jackson's Division at Elizabethton, Carter County, Tennessee, on October 18, 1813 when he was 26 years old. He was discharged on January 17, 1814 at Fish Springs on the Watauga River in Tennessee. The 1830 census shows that in that year, Lawrence Effler and his family were living in what would become Yancey County, North Carolina in 1833. Their daughter, Margaret, was born there. By the 1850 census, all of the family except Lawrence's son Henry had returned to Flag Pond, Tennessee, where they remained until their deaths. Lawrence's sons William, John and George all enlisted in the Confederate Army at Jonesboro, Tennessee, on November 7, 1862. John was captured and died in a Union Hospital in 1863.

Henry Effler married his first cousin, Margaret Grindstaff, and they would live out their lives in Yancey County, N.C. The Efflers and Grindstaffs had intermarried for several generations. Steve Effler's grandmother was Margaret Grindstaff the wife of Henry Effler, his great grandmother was Mary Grindstaff the wife of Lawrence Effler. He was just carrying on a family tradition by marrying one of that name.

The Grindstaffs

In choosing Margaret "Peggy" Grindstaff for his wife, Steve Effler chose a cousin whom he would later claim he barely knew and never did learn to love because she was "too close akin." The Grindstaffs, like the Efflers, trace their family back to Germanic origins and one Dietrich Crantsdorf, born October 3, 1728 in Zweibrucken in what is now Germany. He died in 1789 in Carter County, Tennessee. The Grindstaffs were well represented in western North Carolina as early as 1760, forty-some years before Lawrence Effler arrived from Prussia.

The ill-fated Peggy Grindstaff Effler was born in 1861, the daughter of Joseph and Martha "Patty" Rector Grindstaff. Joseph, born in 1822, was the son of Henry and Cynthia Penland Grindstaff. This Henry Grindstaff, grandfather of Peggy Grindstaff Effler, was the brother of Margaret Grindstaff who married Henry Effler, grandparents of Peggy's husband Steven Effler. The family tree is further entangled because Henry Effler married his first cousin, the niece of his mother, Mary Grindstaff Effler, wife of Lawrence Effler. That young Steven Effler and Peggy Grindstaff were marrying cousins was not an unusual occurrence in those days when cousins were about the only potential spouses available anywhere nearby in those hills and hollers of East Tennessee and Western North Carolina.

Mr. & Mrs. Steve Effler

According to their Yancey County, North Carolina, license, Steve Effler and Peggy Grindstaff were married on March 30, 1879 at Peggy's father's house. They seem to have lived from pillar to post, staying mainly with Steve's mother and grandparents on South Toe River. At the time the 1880 census was taken, however, they were actually living alone in a separate household just four houses from Alexander "Sandy" Patton who would later play a key role in this story and Steve Effler's fate. As in most other official records, Steve's name is spelled "Stephen" in this census. He is listed as 20 years old and his wife, Margaret, is also 20. Their son, Joseph W., is two months old at the time of the census. This son was apparently named for Peggy's father; however, at some point before Effler's hanging, the name was changed to Alfred Erwin. Descendants have no explanation as to why this was done. The child was born on April 28, 1880. When his mother was murdered, he was only eight months old, quite literally still a babe in arms, as he was found alive beside his dead mother, her right arm still enfolding him.

It was in December 1880, just as the dead of winter was coming on, that the young Effler couple and their baby moved into an old log cabin right beside the wagon road on the McDowell side of Buck Creek Gap.

Sifting through the legends

Given the way folklore is embellished with each new telling, it is not surprising that the story of Joshua Young's dream and Steve Effler's hanging have become a kind of fiction. The remarkable thing, I suppose, is that there are any facts at all left inside the story after it had been told and retold for 120 years. In Part IV of this book, five different versions of the story are reproduced either as they were told or as they were written down. Only one of them, Sallie Glenn's account, discounts the part about Josh Young's dream. All of them, even Mrs.

Glenn's, give Joshua credit for stopping the funeral procession that would have buried Peggy Effler. If Steve Effler had succeeded in that, he would also have buried the key evidence of murder—the bruises and broken bones in her body. All of the stories either identify Joshua Young or his friend Sandy Patton as a justice of the peace who had the authority to make an arrest and send for the coroner and the sheriff.

The facts, just the facts

When I first went searching for the trial records of the Effler case, I was disappointed to find nothing in the criminal or superior court records for McDowell County or the state Supreme Court records in the main North Carolina archives building in Raleigh. "Well," an archivist explained, "the more recent records are in the Supreme Court Records Annex." I walked a few blocks and found the small warehouse-like building, with a tiny office up front. It took only a few minutes to find the State v. Effler file, 114 pages of it. I raced through the various documents—subpoenas of witnesses, venires of jurors—looking for the name of my old granddaddy's first cousin. And, sure enough, there it was in the list of witnesses and subpoenas for them to appear at the trial: "Joshua Young." I promptly asked the archivist to Xerox the entire file and mail it to me. I couldn't imagine that a dream could ever have been entered as evidence in a murder trial—even 120 years ago—but for a brief moment, I allowed myself to think the story passed down in our family was all true. There was the name to prove it; and another name from the story, Sandy Patton, was also on the list of witnesses. And the second doctor in the story, Dr. Virgil Butts of Marion, was also listed as a witness. The pieces seemed to be fitting together neatly.

However, once I began to go over the files more carefully, there was nothing neat about them. The pages were in a jumble, totally out of sequence. The defense lawyer and solicitor (prosecutor) had gone through 110 different jurors summoned in two venires before they agreed on a jury of 12 men. There were what appeared to be two separate transcripts of the witnesses' testimony in the trial, neither of them even pretending to be a full verbatim transcript. One of them was rougher than the other and this one I now believe had to be the rough notes taken by the judge. The second, more detailed, set of notes of testimony was apparently the official transcript taken down by the clerk of court or a court reporter.

I began to find contradictions between the documents and the legends immediately. It was also obvious that the jury was hearing all kinds of contradictions between what Steve Effler said he had done and what others claimed to have seen and heard at the scene of the crime. It should be kept in mind that Effler maintained his innocence from the time he was arrested on January 12, 1881 until May 18, 1882, the day before he was hanged when he wrote a full confession of the gory details of his crime.

In the following, I have organized the evidence and reconstructed the crime according to chronology, not as it was presented to the jury, although Ed Sowers was, in fact, the first witness for the state. The entire transcript and the judge's notes will be found in the documents section, Part V, of this book.

Thursday, January 6, 1881

Ed Sowers said at the time of the murder, January 6th, 1881, he was living at the foot of the Blue Ridge on the Yancey County side and Stephen Effler was living a mile and a half from him at the foot of the ridge on the McDowell County side. Steve's grandfather, Henry Effler, also lived on the Yancey side, about a mile from Sowers' place.

That day, January 6th, Sowers had gone over to Marion and was coming back home. It was along about dark when he came to the Efflers' place. Steve was out at the hog pen and yelled for him to stop and rest a spell. Sowers went inside the cabin and found Peggy sitting at the table with the baby in her lap. He asked how she was doing and Peggy said, "I am as well as common." Effler came in and told Peggy to fix supper for Sowers and she did. The three of them then sat for a while, talking before the fire.

Peggy said she wanted to go to her father's house the next day, but Steve said she couldn't go because he had to work at the mill all day. The transcript also says Steve told Sowers, "she said she would lie with him if he wouldn't let her go to her father's." It seems obvious that this should read, "she said she would *not* lie with him…." And this could have been the beginning of the fatal quarrel. Folks in the valley say it all started when Peggy burned the bread that night, but there is no evidence of that.

Sowers said he walked on home and sat up "a right smart while" and then went to bed.

His wife was powerful sick

Steve Effler said he went to bed with his wife about 15 minutes after Ed Sowers left. He said he'd been asleep about a quarter of an hour when Peggy "woke me up pulling my hair and poking about. I pulled her down; asked her what was the matter. She gave no answer. She fell back toward the head of the bed." He couldn't say whether she struck anything; he "didn't hear her head pop." Effler said he then ran to the house of his grandfather, Henry Effler. He was gone about an hour. He swore that Peggy was alive when he left, dead when he came back.

Steve's first cousin, Jeff Lanning, told the court he was staying at his grandfather Henry Effler's house that night. It was about 9 p.m. or later, when Steve Effler came running over and hollered. "I understood him to say Peggy was dead, though the dogs were barking so I wasn't sure what he said. He hollered again and said Peggy was dying."

Jeff's father, Gavan Lanning, said he was also staying at Henry Effler's that night when Steve came over. "The dogs were barking and he hallowed before he got to the house. I was in bed and didn't hear what he said. We told him to come to the house and he came in and said, 'Peggy is about dead and I want you all to go over there.'" When asked what was wrong with his wife, Effler said she'd complained about her head and neck and had a spell like the one she'd had along in the summer.

When they got out in the road, young Lanning asked Steve what Peggy was complaining of. Steve said she said her neck and head were hurting. Now, in some of the legends and in Effler family tradition, it is said that Peggy Effler suffered from asthma. Some said this was why Steve Effler thought he could get away with explaining that his wife had strangled due to a severe attack of asthma. However, nowhere in the court testimony is there any evidence that she suffered from any kind of ailment prior to the murder. In fact, the evidence contradicting that—that she was in good health—surely figured in Effler's conviction.

Ed Sowers said he'd been in bed about an hour when he heard somebody or something running by his house. Somebody called to him from the door, but he didn't answer. It was Steve Effler and four or five of his relatives. Someone yelled again and said for Sowers to get up and go with them because "Steve Effler's wife was powerful sick."

Steve told Jeff Lanning to stay with the women, and he and Sowers would run on ahead. Effler told Sowers that his wife had appeared to be out of her head. She was having a fit or something when he left her.

When they got near the house, Effler seemed scared by some noise. "What is that?" he asked. Sowers said he thought it was the hogs. Effler put his hand on Sowers' shoulder and held onto him as they walked from the fence to the house. He called out, "Oh, Peggy." But there was no answer.

Inside the house, Effler walked toward the bed. Sowers couldn't remember whether he touched his wife's body or not. He turned back to Sowers and said, "She's dead."

"No, surely," said Sowers. "Yes," said Effler, "What will I do?" Sowers said Effler "balled over" and cried "or let on he was crying." Sowers lit the fire. Peggy was on the bed. Sowers could see bloody froth running out of her nose and coming from her mouth. Her face was red and purple, but he did not see any bruises. She was lying on her back, her face toward their eight-month-old baby, her left arm over her breast, her right arm was around the child. She was not wearing the dress she'd been wearing at supper; the only thing she had on was a kind of black sack undergarment and it was pulled up above her waist. Sowers went over to the bed and put his hand on Peggy. She was already getting cold.

Sowers straightened Peggy's head. Her neck was limber, he recalled, it turned very easily. He closed her eyes and mouth. Sowers said he did not touch the body again, but waited for Steve's mother, Polly Effler, and aunt, Catherine Lanning, to dress her.

Steve asked Sowers to see if the child were dead. "I touched it and it woke up," Sowers said. Effler then took the baby.

Friday, January 7

Ed Sowers' wife, Rebecca, said she got up to the Efflers' cabin about three hours after her husband went. That would have been just past midnight and going into Friday morning. She said Peggy was lying on the bed, her nose running with bloody froth. She also noticed two of Peggy's "chemises" hanging up, still damp as if they'd just been washed.

Some time after daylight, Henry Effler got worried that people might say his grandson had killed his wife, so he went and got J.M. Burgin to come and examine her. Burgin said, "I first talked to Stephen—asked him what ailed her. He said she took a spasm or fit and he held on to her until she was disabled…he said she fought him and pulled his hair as long as she was able to do anything and then he laid her on the bed and started for her [sic] grandfather." Burgin said her face was swollen under her eyes, but he didn't examine her neck, he did not try to lift her head.

Jane Johnson said the family also asked her to come stand watch with the corpse. She said she found the body laid out on the bed. Steve's mother, Polly, said to Jane: "I believe that woman's head is busted all to pieces inside for when I move it I hear it scoush in there just like water." She said Peggy's hands were purple on Friday, but had turned black by Saturday; also, the skin under her eyes had turned black by Saturday.

It was a sacred and ancient tradition that neighbors came in and sat up with the family beside the body; several people stayed awake day and night until the body was buried. Ed Sowers said he stayed until daylight the first night, went home, then came back on Friday night and stayed all night; then, came back again on Saturday night.

Saturday, January 8

By Saturday, word had spread among all the kinfolks and neighbors and a real crowd had gathered around the little Effler cabin just over the county line from Buck Creek Gap. Ells and Ruthia Byrd Burnett were among those who came across from the Yancey side to help sit up with the corpse. They lived about 3 miles away. Ells' name comes from an old German surname, it is incorrectly listed as "Eldridge" in several documents apparently because people believed it was a shortened version of the longer name. He said Peggy Effler looked "swelled about her face and mighty dark. I saw Stephen. He appeared to want to hear what was said. He was listening and watching people out of doors."

Ruthy Burnett said Peggy's left jaw and left ear were darker than the rest of her face. "I felt about her head and neck only, [but] found that she was swelled powerful. Her head and shoulders [were] closer together than usual. Her chin stuck towards her breast." She said Steve appeared to be uneasy and would get up any time anybody went to look at his wife's corpse.

By Saturday, Peggy's own family had come from Mitchell County. Although Peggy had been dressed by Steve's mother and aunt, her own mother now took charge and sat beside her. Peggy's father, Joseph Grindstaff, asked Charles and Mary Cresawn to come with him to the Effler's cabin and help bring the body back across the mountain for burial in the family graveyard. Mary Cresawn said she felt over the body's ribs and the left side gave in. She pulled an ear and "it 'peared like her head was loose from her neck. Her stomach was swelled. Her left breast was sunk in." She said Steve's manner was strange "as if he were pestered about something." She remembered seeing a couple of pigs come out from under the house with blood on their noses.

On Saturday night, Charles Cresawn and Peggy's father helped put her body in the casket.

Sunday, January 9

In spite of the gory details recorded above, it seems apparent that although there was some suspicion of foul play, the Grindstaffs and Efflers and all the neighbors seemed to accept Steve's explanation of why Peggy's body was so bruised and battered. And, early on Sunday morning, the little group headed up and over Buck Creek Gap in the Blue Ridge and down the wagon road along South Toe River. Apparently they were carrying the casket on their shoulders. Ed Sowers said Steve himself was helping carry it very carefully, insisting they carry the "head foremost up the mountain, feet foremost down."

When the pathetic little procession reached the house of Alexander "Sandy" Patton, it was stopped. We may never know precisely why and how this happened, but all accounts, and all the evidence, show that Joshua Young and Patton were key figures in stopping and apprehending the murderer, Steve Effler. One of the most fascinating accounts of the murder was written in 1967 by then 85-year-old Sallie Glenn. She was born the year Steve Effler was hanged and grew up hearing about it from her Uncle Ells and Aunt Ruthy Byrd Burnette, who were witnesses at the trial. She also heard about it from her husband, Will Glenn, who at age 12, witnessed the hanging.

Mrs. Glenn claimed she was writing to set the record straight because "from time to time, somebody from the present generation has written a tale about the murder and colored it with a legend of how a justice of the peace, who had dreamed of being appealed to by a woman in distress, discovered Peggy Grindstaff Effler had been done in by her husband." However, even as she is dismissing one "tale" of the supernatural, Mrs. Glenn recounts how Polly Effler stopped the rain with her prayers and how the devil made his appearance that Sunday night in the Toe River Valley.

Of all the published accounts, Mrs. Glenn's has the most details that can be corroborated from other sources. Starting with Ed Sowers' part in the case, she follows much of the evidence produced in the trial—although she had no access to the trial documents.

As Mrs. Glenn told it, her Aunt Ruth Byrd Burnette was the real heroine of the case. When she arrived at the Efflers' cabin, she found clothes packed around the dead Peggy's neck and head. She started to take them away and "Steve's mother Polly told her not to do that, that Peggy had such a pain in her head that her head would not lay straight."

Her Aunt Ruth waited until Polly left the room and then went back to the corpse and removed the padding around the head. As soon as she did, "Peggy's head rolled to one side. Ruth put the clothes back and went to where the men were making the coffin and told them something was bad wrong. Elza [Ells] Burnette rode his mule to Josh Young's in Yancey County, Josh being a J.P., and they went to J.R. [sic] Patton's and there they all decided what to do, knowing they would come by there taking Peggy's body to Red Hill to bury her."

Nearly all accounts agree that the funeral procession was stopped on the road in front of Sandy Patton's house. The site is on the present-day Highway 80 beside Ballew's nursery and greenhouses and the dirt road that leads up to the Patton cemetery, where Sandy and his relatives are buried. From all the evidence, Peggy Effler's casket was moved inside Patton's house and stayed there for two days while the neighbors held Steve Effler as a kind of hostage until justice could be served.

Now, here is something else that all accounts agree on: they all say that either Joshua Young or Sandy Patton or both were justices of the peace. However, I have searched the records in vain and have found no proof of this. Justices of the peace were appointed for life. They were the local magistrates, the law, in fairly large domains. The sheriff and his deputies were usually located in the county seats many miles away. The names of all these magistrates were recorded in Branson's Business Directories published for the whole state in the late 1800s. I checked the directories for 1879 and for 1882 (the intervening years were missing) and found that neither Joshua Young nor Sandy Patton was listed as the justice of the peace in that area.

Furthermore, the justice of the peace who actually signed the warrant for Stephen Effler's arrest was named W.R. Craig.

Sallie Glenn offered one other detail about that day which seems to be supported by the evidence. She said that Jim Westall was deputized to hold Steve Effler and see that he did not run. She wrote: "Jim Westall kept close guard on him and kept one hand in his pocket all the time. Steve and Jim had grown up together and Jim said he knew how far [fast] Steve could run. He said, 'Steve, I know you can run like a deer; as sure as you do, I will kill you.' Steve said, 'I know I am going to be killed, but Jim I don't want you to do it.' They said Steve sat there looking like a wild, scared animal. All the time, Jim didn't have anything in his pocket but a knife…[Steve] acted terrified as if some unseen demon was near him. Some of the witnesses were outside and they said they saw the devil himself, that he was as large as a mule, black as midnight, and about ten feet above the ground, in the air and shaking. Next morning, there was no sign of tracks in the snow—all was smooth."

According to all the accounts passed down in Yancey County, after stopping the funeral procession, Joshua Young called for the Yancey coroner to come examine the body. As the tale is told, the Yancey doctor was afraid of the Efflers and so declared no crime had been committed, saying Peggy Effler had died of natural causes. In fact, a Dr. Whittington of Yancey was subpoenaed as a witness at the trial, but if he testified, it is not recorded. Another man from Yancey named John Simmons was also subpoenaed as a witness. Unfortunately, the only testimony recorded for him is this: "I was on the Yancey Coroner's jury."

The most likely explanation is that the Yancey doctor came and explained that since the crime had been committed in McDowell County, he had no jurisdiction, and so they should call on the authorities in McDowell County. Whatever the reason, that is what they did.

WHAT WAS JOSHUA YOUNG'S ROLE?

We come now to the key point in this story and this book. Did Joshua Young have that dream? Was he, in fact, the one who stopped the funeral procession? As to the first one, I reckon we may never know for sure. However, I firmly believe that Joshua Young himself believed that and told the story that way for the rest of his life. I believe that because that is the way Mrs. Edd Young, told it to me in 1958 and she heard it directly from her husband's uncle, Joshua Young, himself. [Her account, as quoted in my 1959 mimeographed history of the Young family is reproduced in full in Part IV of this book.]

Joshua Young, by every account, was a respected man in the community. He was the son of Wesley and Elizabeth Wilson Young, the grandson of Strawbridge and Martha Wilson Young. Strawbridge Young, son of Thomas and Naomi Hyatt Young, was one of the original European settlers in the Toe River Valley, staking out grants for hundreds of acres of land in the late 1790s and early 1800s in the vast unsettled land along the South Toe River near what is now Micaville and Newdale. Part of this land passed on to his son Wesley and part of that passed on to his son, Joshua.

On October 5, 1868, Joshua Young married a widow named Naomey S. Jameson and they had one child who died in infancy and a daughter, Mary, who would live to maturity only to add a bizarre and tragic postscript to this already tragic drama in the valley. Joshua Young would live on to tell his tale until he died May 24, 1920 and was buried alongside his parents and grand-parents on a hilltop overlooking the Toe River on one side and the Black Mountain Range on the other.

In other words, Joshua Young lived on long enough to tell the story himself to be passed down by generations that overlapped my own. But, what about the facts. We cannot, of course, be certain he had that vision or dream. Nobody could ever prove that, even at that time. In most accounts, Josh Young claimed he had never laid eyes on Peggy Effler before he saw her in the casket that

Sunday and recognized her as the woman with the broken neck who had appealed to him in the dream.

What we do know is that both he and Sandy Patton were summoned as witnesses and both testified in the trial. Although, the judge and the clerk or whoever transcribed the testimony, did a poor job of it, enough survives to confirm some of the legend, at least.

All we have to go on are the following words transcribed from Joshua Young's testimony at the trial: "I noticed the blood from her nose. Noticed a bruise under her left eye & towards her ear. When I raised her her head went back and it seemed to me as if her head went back & struck her back. I told a young man named Jameson & told him to raise her head level with her body. I was confident her neck was broken. Deft. [defendant Steve Effler] was making a fuss. [Several words in the following are illegible.] Didn't see any...He looked scared. Saw him look towards...."

And that is the record, "the facts," as to Joshua Young as they have survived in the records. What stands out is the fact that he alone made a serious examination of the body; he alone said "I was confident her neck was broken." Even long after the fact, even knowing for sure Effler had killed his wife, none of the other witnesses went so far as that. This, in my opinion, confirms Joshua Young's key role in the case and corroborates the key element in the legend.

And, it is a fact that Dr. Virgil R. Butts was summoned from McDowell County to make an official examination of the body. He probably did not arrive at Sandy Patton's house until the next day, Monday, January 10, 1881.

Monday, January 10

Dr. Butts' examination was extensive and proved beyond a doubt that Peggy Effler had been beaten to death. Her neck had been broken; her nose was broken; her 5th, 6th, and 7th ribs on the right side were fractured. He found an incision three inches long and an inch and a half deep on her shoulder and various wounds or bruises on her abdomen. Butts would later testify, "In my opinion these wounds were caused by external violence." He said the wounds could not have been caused by carrying the body in the casket over the mountain.

Apparently, Butts confronted Steve Effler with the facts and Effler more or less admitted he had killed his wife. There is only a vague reference to this in the transcript, unfortunately. Butts says "I talked with Stephen Effler." He said "I sought the conversation." The most incriminating evidence from this conversation was that Effler contradicted his own words and said that his wife had not suffered any kind of fit, her health was generally good. Butts explained that Effler was under arrest at the time and "there were quite a number present" in the room. "It was after the inquest had been held in the next room. There were not over a dozen in the room, most women, his mother among them."

The defense tried in vain to get this evidence suppressed on the grounds that Butts obtained it under duress, that Effler had talked to Butts about killing his wife because he feared for his life. "His appearance was that of one in trouble," said Butts in more polite language. However, a line has been crossed out in the transcript, "when had been threat of mobbing." It seems from other testimony that the crowd was getting agitated and there was talk of lynching or "mobbing" Effler on the spot.

However, based on Butts' examination, a man named S.C. Turner applied to Justice of the Peace W.C. Craig on January 10, 1881 for a warrant to arrest Effler for murder. Craig granted the warrant and McDowell County Sheriff Joe G. Neal deputized S.C. Turner, Merrit Burgin, [name illegible] Patton, and Stickland McFalls to serve the warrant.

Arrested and indicted for murder

The warrant was served on Wednesday, January 12, 1881, and Steve Effler was committed to jail in Marion that same day for trial at the Spring Term of the Superior Court. On opening day of the court, March 28, 1881, the solicitor (as prosecutors were known in those days) J.S. Adams secured an indictment for murder against Steve Effler by the grand jury.

The indictment was remarkably similar, almost identical, to the indictment handed down 50 years earlier against Frankie Silver for the murder of her husband. Both of them adhere to the archaic language of murder indictments from the ancient English Common Law. The Frankie Silver indictment is one sentence of more than 500 words; the solicitor in State v. Effler did have the grace to break the indictment down into several sentences. The indictment is reproduced in full in the documents section of this book.

It read, in part: "The jurors for the State upon their oath present that Stephen Efler [sic] late of the County of McDowell, Laborer, not having the fear of God before his eyes but being moved and seduced by the instigation of the devil on the Sixth day of January in the year of Our Lord One Thousand Eight Hundred and Eighty One with force and arms at and in the county aforesaid in and upon one Peggie Efler [sic] in the peace of God and the state then and there being feloniously willfully and of his malice aforethought did make an assault; and that the said Stephen Efler then and there feloniously willfully and of his malice aforethought—did strike beat kick and choke the said Peggie Efler with both his hand and feet in and upon the head nose neck side and other parts of the body of her the said Peggie Efler...."

The trial

It says something wonderful for our legal system, that even at this early date the trial of a man like Stephen Effler would involve some of the best legal minds in our state. From all accounts, Effler was illiterate and had no money or property at all. And yet, he was represented by James Madison Gudger, a 26-year-old lawyer just beginning a distinguished career that would include being elected to the state senate and the U.S. Congress. Born October 22, 1855, Gudger was the youngest son of Joseph Jackson and Sarah Emeline Barnard Gudger. His grandfather was James Gudger, one of the first European children born west of the Blue Ridge; his grandmother was Annie Love, daughter of Revolutionary soldier, Col. Robert Love. His great grandparents were William and Martha Young Gudger, pioneer settlers in what is now Buncombe County.

The solicitor or prosecutor in the case was Joseph Shepherd Adams, another distinguished lawyer with deep roots in the history of East Tennessee and Western North Carolina. Adams was born October 12, 1840 at Strawberry Plains, Tennessee, the only child of the Rev. Stephen D. and Cordelia Shepherd Adams. His mother was the daughter of Burnsville inn-keeper, Joseph Shepherd, and his wife, Elizabeth Horton, a daughter of Zephaniah Horton, a soldier in the Revolutionary War. The elder Adams met his wife while serving as a Methodist circuit rider on a visit to Burnsville. They later returned to Burnsville and established the Burnsville (Methodist) Academy, whose success caused the Baptists to establish a rival school that would become Mars Hill College.

Judge Jeter C. Pritchard praised Adams' work as a solicitor: "During his term of office as solicitor he had frequent opportunities to oppress and wrong the poor and ignorant who were brought before him for prosecution; but never once did he allow the hope of reward or personal enmity to influence him in the discharge of his duty. Neither did he ever permit himself to be influenced by the fear of evil consequences to himself or his fortunes while he was a solicitor. He showed no man any favor because of social or political influence. He did his duty simply and faithfully, without fear and without favor and when his career as prosecuting officer expired he had, perhaps, as few enemies among those upon whom the punishment of the law had fallen through his efforts as a prosecuting attorney as any other man who ever held that important office." Adams would go on to serve as a Superior Court Judge until his death April 2, 1911.

Steve Effler's trial was originally scheduled to begin in the spring term, 1881, of Superior Court in McDowell County. However, Effler and his lawyer successfully petitioned the court for a postponement to the fall term in order to give them more time to prepare their case. At the fall term, yet another distinguished legal figure, Augustus Sherrill Seymour, would be the judge presiding over the trial that determined whether Steve Effler lived or died. Seymour was born November 30, 1836 in Ithaca, New York, into a family that included New York Gov. Horatio Seymour. He came to North Carolina as a carpetbagger, settling in New Bern in 1864 and being admitted to the state bar in 1866. According to William Powell's Encyclopedia of North Carolina Biography, Seymour would live to overcome the taint of being a carpetbagger and rise to prominence in the North Carolina legal system the hard way: "...amid difficult times, his marked ability, honest and sympathetic character, and considerate and kindly personality endeared him to the New Bernians who returned home after the war. During corruptible eras his reputation remained untarnished." He was elected to the State House in 1868, the State Senate in 1872. He was named a superior court judge in 1874, his term ending in 1882 when he was named a judge in the U.S. District Court by President Chester A. Arthur. He served as a federal judge until his death in 1897.

The trial of Stephen Effler in 1881 offers some striking contrasts with the murder trial of Frankie Silver in 1831. Because none of the testimony at Ms. Silver's trial has survived, we have only hints from other documents as to what evidence was presented at the trial. Serious questions about that trial may never be answered—most intriguingly, why the jurors changed from a vote of

9-3 for acquittal to unanimous for guilt. However, the most striking difference is that Frankie Silver was not allowed to go on the stand and tell her side of the story. At the height of the Watergate hearings for the impeachment of President Nixon, U.S. Sen. Sam Ervin answered a letter from me about this case. Ervin was born just a few blocks from the spot where Frankie was hanged He told me his daddy told him that the clerk of court, Burgess Gaither, told him that Frankie would definitely have been acquitted if she'd been able to go on the stand and explain how her husband had abused her and how she had killed him in self defense. Under the laws of that time, again strictly adhering to the English Common Law, the accused was deemed an incompetent witness and could not testify under any circumstances.

By 1881, the law had been changed. As now, the accused could not be compelled to testify against himself. However, if he chose to do so, he could take the stand in his own defense. No doubt, to his regret, Stephen Effler chose to do just that. Just as Frankie Silver's truths might have convinced a jury to save her, you get the feeling the jury saw right through the lies Effler told when he took the stand.

More important, by deciding to become a witness, Effler allowed a whole area of negative testimony that would otherwise have been inadmissible. Like any other witness, he was now subject to testimony that would "impeach" or question the truth of his testimony and evidence could also be presented as to his character—or lack thereof.

Ed Sowers told the court that Effler had told him two years before that he wasn't going to live with his wife. He "said she was as good to him as to a baby. That the reason he wasn't going to live with her was because he didn't love her." Effler's cousin Jeff Lanning said he heard Steve and Peggy quarreling one night and also said Steve talked about leaving her. Peggy's father, Joseph Grindstaff, said, "I was there a time when they wouldn't sleep together. He wouldn't carry the child." The father-in-law also said that Steve would "take off with other young boys. He went off a while about three weeks or so." Jane Johnson said Steve and Peggy "didn't get along very good. Don't think he treated her as a man ought to his wife. He didn't go to preaching together. One time they didn't sleep together."

Peggy's sister, Martha Grindstaff, said she stayed with the young couple for a month. She said Steve just took off when the baby was born. She said she didn't know what the trouble was, but Steve wouldn't even get his wife anything to eat when she was sick.

Although some people dismiss "circumstantial evidence," that is almost always the only kind of evidence you have in murder trials. It is extremely rare that eye-witnesses can be found to murders. The circumstantial evidence against Steve Effler in this case was overwhelming, although he persisted in saying he was not guilty.

Speaking in his own defense, Stephen Effler told the court he and his wife had been asleep "about an hour" when "she woke me up pulling my hair and poking about. I pulled her down and asked her what was the matter. She gave no answer. I then went to grandfathers. When I came back she was dead." On cross-examination by the solicitor, he said, "I went to bed about 15 minutes after Sowers left. I had been asleep about a quarter of an hour when she woke me up. She fell back towards head of the bed, don't know whether she struck anything, didn't hear her head pop, didn't hear her strike anything."

However, with the expert testimony of Dr. Virgil R. Butts, the state was able to prove that Peggy Effler's injuries were far too severe to have happened as the result of a fall, even if she were suffering from convulsions. They also had Butts' expert testimony on that subject and this would become one of the key points in Effler's appeal to the Supreme Court.

After examining the body at Sandy Patton's house, Dr. Butts testified he confronted Effler on this very point about his wife's health. "I asked him if she (his wife) ever had fits. He said no. I asked him if her health was generally good. He said yes—excepting that she could not occasionally eat breakfast." Through his lawyer, Effler would try to claim that he had made this confession under duress. A crowd had gathered as the doctor examined the body and he was afraid they might hang him on the spot. Sandy Patton had, in fact, testified that "there was considerable excitement in the crowd and that something had been said about mobbing the prisoner—but that he had not heard anything of the kind said in prisoner's hearing or know of anything of the kind said in his presence."

In writing the later appeal, Judge Seymour gave this summary of the facts in the case: "The deceased and defendant were husband and wife and lived alone—a baby of 8 months with them—in a log house on the south side of the foot of the Blue Ridge. A neighbor eat supper with them on the night of the alleged homicide and a little while after dark left them and went home—about a mile and a half off on the other side of the mountain. An hour or so afterwards he was awakened by def. [defendant] who said his wife was very badly off. He and a number of others went with deft. Home—and found deceased dead. Dr. Butts testified that her neck was broken, three of her ribs were broken, her shoulder out of joint, bruises on her abdomen and an incised... [incision] 3 inches long and one inch deep on her right shoulder. She was found lying on the bed, her head turned partly towards her baby—a sack on but no 'shirt.' Her wet 'shirts' were hung up in the room to dry. No blood found on her person save some in her nostrils and mouth. The theory of the defense was that she had a fit and fell over the bed and broke her neck. Deft. Had told a witness J.M. Burgin so he testified that deceased had a spasm or fit & he held her until she was disabled & then he went to his grandfathers & Ed Sowers said she had something like fits."

The solicitor was thus able to knock down Effler's testimony about his wife's "fits," he was also able to suggest that Effler had washed his wife's "chemises" or "shirts" to get the blood out and then hung them up to dry. Apparently, the bloody water drained through the floor boards and left puddles under the house. The last witness for the state, Mary Cresawn, said she heard a noise from some animals under the house, then she saw two pigs come out with red blood on their noses.

Even with one of the brightest and best lawyers in western North Carolina representing him, Steve Effler's lies could not hold up in the face of such testimony. On October 25, 1881, the jury found him guilty and he was sentenced to be hanged on "Friday, 11th day of November, 1881, on which day between the hours of eleven and two o'clock he shall be taken thence to the place of execution appointed by law and there be hanged by the neck until he be dead."

Appeal to the State Supreme Court

Effler's lawyer immediately filed notice of appeal to the North Carolina Supreme Court so the hanging was automatically postponed. Noting that he was impoverished and had no funds to pay a bond for an appeal, the judge granted him an appeal without giving security. The judge's appeal carefully noted and explained in detail all four of the exceptions to his rulings which Effler's lawyer had made during the trial.

The North Carolina Supreme Court also carefully considered every one of these points. James M. Gudger was allowed to argue his case in person before the state's highest court. Writing for the Court, Justice Thomas Ruffin (1824-1889) began his opinion with these words, "Impressed as we were with the earnestness of counsel who argued the cause before us, and realizing the immense importance to the prisoner of the issues involved, we have bestowed upon them our most earnest consideration."

The higher court found that there was no legal basis for any of the errors cited by the defense. The first one had to do with a potential juror who admitted he had an opinion on the case. However, the defense refused to ask what that opinion was. Justice Ruffin said the defense was obliged to find out if the potential juror's opinion was prejudiced for or against his client.

The second "error" cited by Effler's lawyer had to do with the testimony against Effler's character. The court ruled: "Where the defendant in a criminal action avails himself of the act of 1881, Ch. 110, and becomes a witness in his own behalf, he thereby subjects himself to all the disadvantages of that position, in the same manner as any other witness, and may be discredited by proof of his general bad moral character."

The third point of appeal had to do with the statements Effler had made to Dr. Butts. The court ruled "Whether the declarations of a prisoner are voluntary or induced, by hope or fear, is a question of fact to be decided by the court below, whose finding is conclusive. And the mere fact of the prisoner's making them while under arrest is not in law sufficient to exclude his declarations otherwise freely made."

The fourth point had to do with Mary Cresawn's testimony about the pigs with bloody noses. The defense had not objected to this testimony at the time, but asked that it be stricken the next day of trial on the grounds of irrelevancy. The higher court ruled there was no error because "it is a matter within the discretionary power of the Judge, and its exercise is not reviewable."

Concluding for the court, Justice Ruffin ruled: "We find nothing in the case of which the prisoner can justly complain. He was tried by a jury fairly selected, and the law governing his case rightly administered." The judgment of the Superior Court was affirmed, which meant that the execution of Steve Effler could now proceed back in McDowell County.

At the Spring Term of the Superior Court in McDowell County, it was ordered: "Judgment of the Court, that the said Stephen Efler [sic] be remanded to the custody of the Sheriff of McDowell County to be kept by him safely and confined in the jail of said County, until Friday the 19th day of May 1882, on which day between the hours of Eleven O'Clock A.M. and Two O'Clock P.M., he take the said Stephen Efler from said Jail and hang him by the neck until he be dead. May the Lord have mercy upon his soul."

Effler and his lawyer would make one last desperate effort to save him from the gallows. They went into the court and "counterfeited insanity," as the lawyer would phrase it in the document referred to in the following paragraphs. There was a hearing before a judge and the court ruled that Stephen Effler was not insane; he knew what he was doing when he killed his wife and he was fully aware of the punishment he was about to receive.

May 18, 1882: Stephen Effler's Confession

[Author's note: Some time in the year 2000, I wrote a letter to the editor of the Mitchell County News asking for information about the Steve Effler case. From that, I began an extensive correspondence by e-mail and regular mail with Hazel Hollifield, whose great grandmother was Steve Effler's mother's sister, Katherine, who married Gavan Lanning. At some point, Hazel Hollifield mentioned that she had a letter that was supposed to have been written by Effler himself. She had gotten it from Anita Justice Collins Wages, Effler's great granddaughter. I was skeptical, but wildly curious to see what she had.

[What she sent me was a Xerox copy of a handwritten document 15 pages long. To put it mildly, it was one of the most chilling pieces of writing I had ever read and I have been collecting such things for most of my 60-some years. It was obviously not written by Effler himself, but must have been written by his lawyer. In the text, Effler claims he has educated himself while in prison, but the reader will also note the writing switches from the third to the first person several times. And in the very middle of the confession, the real author chooses to delete whatever it was Effler intended to say about those who had testified against him in the trial. Having said that, however, there is no question in my mind that the document is an authentic confession by Effler. We have been able to corroborate nearly every single detail he mentions with other sources.

[Such a confession, of course, was part of the ritual that preceded a hanging. In fact, there was by tradition a point when the condemned man or woman was asked on the scaffold if he or she had any final words to say, and they nearly always did. The doomed man's confession of his guilt was also a traditional source of broadsides and ballads going back to ancient England that served as warnings among the religious—if you sin as this man did, you, too, will suffer the consequences. Sadly, the ghastly details of Effler's crime left nothing whatever to sing about; in fact, if it hadn't been for the story of Joshua Young's dream, this tragic story might never have been popularized in Appalachian folklore as it has been. Here, then, after all the lies, is the truth about what Steve Effler did that night as only the man himself could have told it. The notes at the beginning are part of the original document.]

Confession of
Stephen G. Effler In jail

Marion, McDowell Co. N.C. Monday morning, May 18,1882

Born in Cherokee County, Tennessee. At the age of ten years (10) moved to Mitchell Co. N.C. Married to Margaret Grindstaffe [sic] about March 1st 79
Killed his wife Jan. 6, 81 (1881) in McDowell Co. where he had been living about a month. Arrested Jan. 10th 81. Tried and convicted at fall term 1881 of McDowell Superior Court. Sentenced to be hanged Appealed to Supreme Court Judgment Confirmed. Counterfeited insanity Verdict of Jury
Sentenced at Spring Term 1882 to be hanged May 19, 1882

As I am condemned to be hanged and must soon appear before my God I think it nothing but right and justice from various rumors and reports that have gone out throughout the country to give the public a sketch of my life, and of the crime which I am guilty of. I was born in Cherokee Co. Tenn. And left there when a small child and was brought to Mitchell Co. N.C. at the age of (10) and lived there until about one month before I was put in jail. I lived in McDowell when arrested for this crime.

I was raised by Henry Effler and Peggy Effler, my grandfather & grandmother and also by my mother Polly Effler as they all lived together. I was raised by poor onest [honest] uneducated parents. Though unlearned as they were, they always gave me good advice. If I had only taken this advice I would not have been here today a doomed man. I have never tried to get any person into any difficulty with me, though I was always a rude rattling boy though I never committed any other great crime but this one which I stand charged with of which I am guilty.

I have been in jail this four hundred and ninety two (492) days. I have learned since I have been in jail in the way of education more than any of my people except one, Aunt Martha M. Effler. I was married to Margaret Grindstaffe [sic] about first (1) of Mar. 1879. In my nineteenth year. She was my cousin. I never went to see my wife but twice until we was married. But I always knew her from childhood and knew her to be a good Christian hearted woman. We lived with my grandfather about one year after we were married and then moved to our selves about one mile from grandfathers in Yancey Co.

We lived together there about two months and then moved back to my grandfathers and stayed there until we moved over into McDowell Co.

I would some times go off and when I come back home would tell my wife that I had been off after other women. She would laugh and say she did not care. She did not believe it neither was it so, I just told her so to see what she would say. The great misfortune is I never loved my wife when I married her neither could I learn to love her. She was too near akin.

I would go off and stay and come back to see if I could learn to love her but I never could. The last trip I took off was to Flagpond Tenn. To a Baptist association about Sixty miles from home. I stayed off about one week. I went off once before that to Madison Co. N.C. and got a job of work from Cling. Haney. I made him three thousand rails. I was gone that trip about one month. My wife stayed with my grandfather on all three trips I took except when I went to Flagpond, that time she went to her fathers and stayed.

Now in all my travels I have wished that I had never married her. I have stopped when going to my work and make wishes that I never had married her and would not have begrudged thousands of dollars that I had not, though she was kind to me only at times when I would get to plagering [sic] her she would get mad and try to scratch herself.

We have one child named Alfred Erwin Effler now about two years old. Oh! May he be trained up in the nurture and admonition of the Lord. I will now tell you about how the witnesses swore who swore truth and who swore false. Here he [sic] accused some half dozen witness of false swearing. [NOTE: It is obvious that whoever was helping him write this here deleted everything bad he had to say about those who testified against him.] I think the balance of the witnesses swore against me. Swore the truth so far as they knew.

I told false my self in this case to shun the law. I will now tell you why I killed my wife and how I killed her. I couldn't love her and the devils temptation was so great it seemed I did not want to live with her any longer and on the 6 day of Jan. 1881 Ed Sowers had been to Marion and came in hearing of my house and hollered he was afraid of my dog. I went out and asked him to come in and he came in. said he was very tired. I asked him to eat supper and he sat down and ate supper and stayed about (1) one hour then left.

The devil's temptation came upon me. My wife went to bed about half an hour before I did. I had worked hard that day and lay down on a sheep skin before the fire and rested there. It seemed that the devil had shown me a plan how to get rid of my wife, So I could go back to live with my grandfather. So I took up this plan. After laying on the sheep skin, about (1) one half hour I got up and got me a white strip of cloth about one foot long and went to bed to my wife where she was laying asleep with her face toward the wall. I lay there about one half hour studying how to commit the deed. At last I ran the cloth around under her neck. After the devil had tempted me so great it seemed like he told me I could get out of it if I did do it. I turned over to her and sorter twisted the cloth a-round her neck, I then put knees against her back and pulled it and she sprang out of the bed with me on the floor. We fell among some benches there. I held to her by the cloth around her neck until I found she was dead.

She died without a struggle. Any way after I found she was dead, I pick her up and laid her on the bed. I then ran to the fire and said Lord have mercy on me, what made me do this what will be come of me now. I then got my shoes and ran to my grandfathers and as I went I fixed up a tale to tell then when I got in sight of my grandfathers I hollered and told them my wife was dead then I caught my self, next time told them she had a hurting in her head and was dying then one of my aunts and two of my cousins come with me back home also Ed Sowers come with us. I told them the same tale I had to told my grandfather. When we got back my wife was laying just as I had left her.

My people have been accused of knowing about the case or of its being made known to them but they are clear of the charge, they knew nothing of it neither do they know to this day how it was or why it was. My wife was a good religious woman and I believe she is gone to Heaven. She was so easy killed I am bound to believe it was her astored [sic] way to go. And that she is in heaven to day. Had I been educated this deed would not have been committed and to day I might not have been [one or two lines have either been erased or inked out; it looks like a tear in the original page   ]

My mother told me about two weeks before I married not to marry oh! That I had taken her advice. I may add more to this if not this is the end

Stephen G. Effler

The Hanging

I have scoured the newspapers that existed in the area at the time of the hanging, but have been able to find only one mention at all of Steve Effler's trial or hanging. This was in the *Lenoir Topic* for May 24, 1882. It read: "Stephen Effler, the wife murderer, was hanged in Marion, N.C., last Friday in the presence of a crowd estimated at 5,000. He confessed that he had strangled his wife while asleep in bed and broke her neck. He talked for an hour before he was executed."

The only other account I have found is Sallie Glenn's in 1967 in The McDowell News. Although she was born the same year as the hanging, her husband, Will, was 12 years old at the time and was taken by his father, David M. Glenn, "to see Effler hung."

As Will Glenn would later tell it, he and his 10-year-old brother, Wash, were standing up in a wagon so they could see the scaffold. Will said that Effler was dressed in a white linen vest or jacket. When it came time for them to cut the rope that dropped the trap door under Effler, little Wash lay down on the wagon bed and covered his head.

At the time this article was published in 1967, Bynum G. Finley was 87 years old and still owned the old jail records kept by his father, A.L. "Fate" Finley. The elder Finley had been jailer from 1879 for two terms under Sheriff Joe Neal. Effler rated two lines in the book: "Steve Effler committed to jail 12th January 1881. Released 19th May 1882. Hung."

Bynum Finley also remembered that Sheriff Neal and two of his deputies came to his father and tried to get him to be the executioner. "Fate," the sheriff said, "we've got a job to do today. We've got to hang Effler." But Finley's daddy said, "Ain't no we in this. You're the sheriff." The sheriff then got a man named Landis from Dysartsville to be in charge of the hanging.

According to Mrs. Glenn, the scaffold was erected near where the old Drexel furniture factory stood outside Marion. Bynum Finley said his daddy told him there was such a crowd "it looked like John Robinson's Circus."

Apparently, the Grindstaffs did finally get Peggy Effler's body back to Red Hill and buried it. But, nobody seems to know for sure where the unmarked grave is located. According to family tradition, Steve was buried beside his grandparents at the old cemetery, called Leefield, near Busick in Yancey County, N.C., not far from where the funeral procession was stopped and Steve Effler was held until he could be arrested, tried and hanged for his foul deed. In 2004, Effler's descendants erected a tombstone over the grave believed to be his.

A Tragic Postcript

As if this dreadful story were not tragic enough, Joshua Young was to live to experience yet another wife murder, this one quite literally much closer to home. Joshua and his wife, Naomey, had only one child who lived to maturity, a daughter named Mary who was born in 1870. According to Claudia Young Dellinger, daughter of Mary's first cousin, Ed Young, Mary Young grew into an exquisitely beautiful young woman. She married Thomas H. Ballew, eight years her senior, whose parents Jason and Emily McCanless Ballew had settled just up the valley from the Young family property.

According to Young family legend handed down to Claudia Dellinger, Tom Ballew was intensely jealous of his wife from the beginning. They had four children: Walter, born in September of 1890, John S., born in February of 1892, Cora E., born in June of 1893, and Horace, born in May of 1895. As Claudia told the story to me, Mary Young Ballew was sitting in the window, nursing the baby Horace. Her husband came at her in a jealous rage and shot her in the head at point-blank range.

The Ballews, needless to say, tell a very different story. According to them, the beautiful Mary was "sexing around" with other men and Tom found out about it. There was one man in particular. One day when Tom was supposed to be off working, he came home early to find his wife in bed with this other man. He did nothing to the offending male intruder, but shot and killed his wife on the spot.

The sheriff obviously felt the killing was a clear case of justifiable homicide. I can find no record that any charges were ever brought against Tom Ballew for the murder of his wife. In the 1900 census, Ballew is listed as the head of household with no wife and the four children born to Mary.

On December 15, 1900, Tom Ballew married a second time to a widow named Bessie Gibbs, the daughter of James and Delia McDowell. They would become the parents of seven children—Nola, Virgie, Bonnie, Robert, Woodrow, Lee, Mamie and Edith Ballew. Tom Ballew would live on until February 23, 1935, when he would be buried in the old Patton cemetery alongside his mother, Emily, 1829-1915, and his daughter, Cora, 1894-1922.

Handsome tombstones mark the graves of Tom Ballew and others in his family. Alexander M. "Sandy" Patton's grave is also marked by a nicely engraved stone with his birth and death dates, October 13, 1854-September 28, 1933. Joshua Young's grave is located near his parents and grandparents in the old Strawbridge Young cemetery. And, it, too, is marked by a handsomely engraved stone.

No engraved tombstones mark the graves of Peggy Grindstaff Effler or of Mary Young Ballew. Nobody knows for sure where they were buried.

III. Illustrations

Superior Court order for the sheriff to take Stephen Effler from the jail "and hang him by the neck until he be dead. May the Lord have mercy upon his soul."

Alfred Erwin and Maebelle Hughes Effler

Alfred Effler was an 8-month-baby when his father left him in his dead mother's arms. Shown here as an adult with his wife, he grew up to sire a large family of his own and restore some dignity to the name. Stephen Effler must have had the same dark, lean good looks as his son pictured here and his half-brother on the next page.

Stephen Effler's kinfolks

Top Photo: The family of Stephen Effler's half-brother, Joseph Effler. Children in front: Allie and Beulo Effler; adults, from left: Cline Jones, Joseph Effler, Darcus Ratliff Effler, Meldia Effler, Vester Effler, Millie Effler, Ellis Effler, and Mary Jane Ratliff. Photo at left shows Stephen Effler's aunt, Katharine Effler Lanning and her husband, Francis Govan Lanning. Both were witnesses at his trial.

"I was convinced that her neck was broken…"

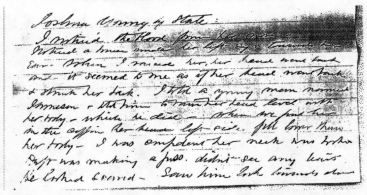

These rough notes are all that survived from Joshua Young's testimony at the
murder trial of Stephen Effler.

Tombstone erected by descendants over Stephen Effler's grave in Leefield Cemetery
at Busick, N.C.

"As I am condemned to be hanged..."

> As I am condemned to be
> hanged and must soon
> appear before my God I
> think it nothing but right
> and justice from various
> rumors and reports, that have
> gone out throughout the
> country to give the public
> a sketch of my life, and of the
> crime which I am guilty
> of. I was born in
> Cherokee Co. Tenn. and left
> there when a small child
> And was brought to Mitchell
> Co. N.C. at the age of (10)
> and lived there until about
> one month before I was put
> in jail. I lived in

Page One of Stephen Effler's Confession. Note: there was a page of factual
information preceding this page.

"She was so easy killed…"

Last page of Stephen Effler's confession. "I may add more to this if not this is the
end. Stephen G. Effler."

IV. Five Versions of the Story

1. From the Young Family History published in mimeographed form by Perry Deane Young at age 18 in 1959. [The author confesses to making many historical errors in the piece. What can I say? I was very young. And I have tried to do better in later years.]

"JOSHUA YOUNG: b. February 14, 1841; d. May 24, 1920; m. Naomey S. Jameson, October 5, 1868.
   issue of Joshua and Naomey Jameson Young:
   5-161—Mary Young; m. Tom Ballew

From this son of Wesley and Elizabeth Wilson Young comes a tale which is told perhaps more even than the tale of Frankie Silver. This story has been published many times in newspapers of the area; Monroe Thomas wrote a version of an eye-witness account in manuscript form; "But," says Mrs. Ed Young, "They all tell it wrong! The way I've heard old Joshua tell it, and I guess I heard it a hundred times, is this: Josh had just got into bed, not asleep, just laying there, when he saw this vision right in front of him. In this vision, Steve Effler's wife begged for Josh to help her. Her head was rolling around as if her neck had been broken.

Well, he tried to roll over and go to sleep, but every time he looked up, the same vision appeared. So, finally he woke his wife up, and she said, 'Aw Josh, yer just a dreamin'. Finally, after he saw he couldn't sleep, he got up and stirred the fire. The next morning he walked down to this old feller's that made caskets, I think his name was Joe Murphy. When he got there Joe had just finished a casket; when Josh asked who had died in the neighborhood, the casket maker replied that Steve Effler's wife had died the night before and was to be buried that afternoon. On hearing this, Joshua replied, 'She didn't die, she was murdered.'

'Josh, what are you a talkin' about, them Efflers'll kill you,' said the casket maker. Later in the day, Joshua walked up to his neighbor John Patton's. There he told Patton all about his dream and Patton replied as the casket maker had. While Joshua was at Patton's, the funeral procession came into view. Joshua persuaded Patton, a Justice of the Peace, to hold the funeral party until a coroner could examine the body. The Yancey coroner came, took a quick look at the body, and said she had died a natural death. Joshua, realizing that the Yancey coroner had said this because he was afraid of the Efflers, sent for a Dr. Cheek (Some say he was Dr. Butts) from McDowell County. After this doctor from McDowell had made a thorough examination of the body, he said that she had died from a broken neck. Now, when Steve Effler heard this he began to cry and say it couldn't be; then when he tried to make his escape, the neighbors helped hold him until the sheriff came."

Steve Effler was hung at Morganton. In Monroe Thomas's account is a legend that when they took his body from the scaffold, he had died, not from a broken neck as his wife had, but from strangulation; the way he had planned for his wife to die. One concludes that fate sometimes runs a weird course; Joshua Young's daughter, Mary Young, was killed by her husband, Tom Ballew.

[One can also conclude that a young fellow like I was at the time can make a heap of mistakes in one short article. To correct just a few of them: Effler was hanged at Marion, not Morganton; the McDowell County coroner's name was Dr. Butts, not Cheek; Joshua Young's neighbor's name was "Sandy" (for Alexander) Patton, not John. And the significance of Effler's death by strangulation was that hanging was supposed to break the neck and thus cause a quicker, and, some felt, more humane death.]

2. Aunt Zona's Version of the Story

[Note: the following is taken from a wonderful book titled, "Aunt Zona's Web."
© 1962 by Arizona Hughes and Thomas C. Chapman. The book grew out of
the correspondence between a young Thomas Chapman in California and
Mrs. J.P. (Arizona) Hughes in Avery County, N.C. Chapman had published a
letter in the Tri-County News in 1956 asking for help in writing a history of his
Wiseman ancestors. Aunt Zona, whose mother was a Wiseman, responded and
the two began a long and affectionate exchange which resulted in the
published story of her life. Among the stories Aunt Zona talked about were two
of the Toe River Valley's most lurid murders—Frankie Silver's axe murder of
her husband; and Josh Young's dream about Steve Effler's murder of his wife,
Peggy. Like so many storytellers before and since, she tied the two horror
stories together, even though they were separated by 50 years and the only real
connection was that they took place only a few miles apart along the Toe River.
Honest to a fault, Aunt Zona admits there were many versions of the stories
and she may not have all the details right. In fact, Frankie Silver was not the
first woman hanged in North Carolina and her story had nothing whatever to
do with the black delta blues ballad of "Frankie and Johnny," although most
people in the area shared Aunt Zona's version until very recently. Arizona
Hughes was born September 24, 1876, so she would have been five and six
years old when the Effler murder and hanging took place. The story is
reprinted here with permission from the publisher, the Puddingstone Press,
Lees-McRae College, Banner Elk, N.C.]

Speaking of winter and snow piled up against the house brings to my mind a
favorite pastime from the days of yore. Entertainment had to come from the
people themselves; there were no radios or televisions. Singing to the accom-
paniment of a banjo filled many a winter evening. Often the old mountain
stories were told between songs. I have heard so many versions of some of
these old stories that at times I could hardly recognize them. Frankie and
Johnny, made famous in song and story, is one of the best known stories from
these hills. Frankie Silvers was the first woman hung in North Carolina—
which is quite a distinction! She lies buried not far from here. The story has
been told in so many ways that even the names have been changed, for Johnny
wasn't a Johnny at all—his name was Charlie, and he wasn't killed with a gun;
he was killed with an ax. At any rate, that is the way it is told in this region, and
it was there along the Toe River, that they lived.

Another story that has fewer versions and has been told many times both in print and by word of mouth is the Steve Effler Murder. The version I have held to be closest to the truth is the one about the Justice of the Peace's dream. My father was acquainted with the Justice, whose name was Josh Young. The ensuing paragraphs give one of the more popular versions, but since time has dulled my memory, I am not sure if this is exactly the way my father told me the story.

This tragic story happened when I was a small girl. Steve Effler and his wife lived in the region of Buck Creek Gap, on the McDowell County side just below the present underpass of the Blue Ridge Parkway—remains of their cabin may still be seen near the present State Highway 80 which winds up Buck Creek Canyon.

Josh Young was a Justice of the Peace in Yancey County for many years during my father's life time. One night he had a horrible dream. He dreamed that a beautiful young woman came running to him for help; her throat was covered with bruises and she was desperate with fright. The dream was so vivid that Josh was awakened and had a difficult time returning to sleep. When he finally managed to fall asleep the same dream came back—exact in every detail.

The next day Josh Young went to his neighbor, "Sandy" Patton, and told him about the dream. It seemed so real that he felt compelled to tell someone. Later in the afternoon of the same day, both Young and Patton noticed a funeral procession making its way down the mountain path that passed their farms. They hadn't heard of anyone dying in the neighborhood, so as the procession approached they asked who had died. Thereupon, the small group of mourners stopped to rest and they unfolded the story. They said that the coffin held the body of a young woman, Mrs. Steve Effler, who had suddenly died the past night. They told how Effler, the young husband, had come to neighbors in the middle of the night to tell them that his wife was very sick, and that he needed help. But! upon returning to the Effler cabin they discovered the woman was dead. Her body was still warm and her little baby was asleep beside her.

The neighbors sent a messenger to the other side of the mountain to tell the parents of the young wife, and to ask them to have a grave ready in the family cemetery. It was also told that the young husband, "overwrought" with grief, wouldn't allow anyone to touch the body. He insisted on preparing her for burial himself.

As the story unfolded, Young was thinking of his dream. He had never seen Mrs. Effler; could it be, that she was the beautiful young woman who came to him in that dream? Was it grief that made the husband want to prepare the body for burial himself? With these thoughts in mind Young asked if the body had been examined by a doctor. The neighbors answered that it had not, so over the protestations of husband and neighbors Josh Young, using his authority as Justice of the Peace, demanded to view the body.

The coffin was taken to Patton's house, as it was the nearest. When it was opened Josh Young was amazed to see the same young woman who had appeared to him in his dream. Thus, he ordered that a doctor be brought from Burnsville, for they had crossed into Yancey County for the burial. Effler was almost in a rage, but there was nothing he could do. The doctor arrived and made a rapid examination; his conclusion was that the woman had died of natural causes. Effler, of course, was triumphant, but Josh Young was not satisfied. He told the husband and mourners that an examination would have to be made by a doctor from McDowell County where the death occurred. He sent word to Marion in McDowell County and Dr. Butt [sic] and the sheriff of McDowell came. Unlike the other doctor, Dr. Butt had the body removed from the coffin and place on a table. He made a complete examination; whereupon, he announced that Mrs. Effler had died from strangulation, and also that her neck had been broken.

The sheriff arrested the husband and took him to Marion to jail; however, the husband continued to declare his innocence.

The following day the sheriff and a group of men went to the Effler cabin to look for some evidence of violence. None could be found, and they were about to leave when one of the men commented about how loose some of the floor boards were. It was also pointed out that the loose boards were clean and unworn while the boards adjoining them were worn and discolored from use. The men decided to investigate and upon turning the boards over; it was discovered that they were stained with blood.

When Effler was confronted with this evidence he confessed; he related how he had quarreled with his wife and while in a rage he had knocked her to the floor and twisted a cloth around her throat. He twisted the cloth until her neck broke and blood gushed from her mouth and nostrils onto the floor. He was able to place his wife in bed and fool the neighbors, but in his haste he hadn't taken the time to nail the boards securely to the floor joists; he was principally concerned with concealing the blood and disposing of any signs of a struggle.

The jury brought in a verdict of guilty and Steve Effler was hung. Although the trial was held in mid-June a storm came and snow was reported to have fallen on many of the higher parts of the mountains. The log cabin, in which the crime was committed, was never occupied again. It gradually fell into ruins and now very little remains to remind us of the people who once lived there, but I am sure their sad story will be continued down through the ensuing generations by those who live in these hills."

3.   Sallie Glenn's version of the Steve Effler murder story

Story in The McDowell News, 1967:

[Photo Caption] MRS. SALLIE GLENN, who was 85 January 5, is the mother of former Sheriff Frank D. Glenn and Howard Glenn of Marion and makes her home with the Howard Glenns on Jacktown Road. She also has a daughter, Mrs. Ethel Carpenter of Denton, Montana and Colorado Springs, and a step-daughter, Mrs. G.C. Stamey of Marion.

A widow since she was 49 years old, Mrs. Glenn has spent much time out west in California and Montana and has visited in Tiawana [sic], Mexico. Since re-settling in Marion she still keeps occupied. "I guess I've made 75 bonnets, and a sight of aprons," she says. She has been called on many times for the story of the famous Effler murder which resulted in this county's only legal hanging. (Photo by Jim Pettit).

Mrs. Sallie Glenn Tells of 1881 Murder
That Led to County's Only Legal Hanging

by Rosamond Braly

McDowell County, it is said, has had only one legal hanging.

It's been 85 years since Steve Effler was hanged on May 19, 1882 in Marion for killing his wife, January 6, 1881. But the details of the murder—as she heard them in her childhood—are still fresh in the memory of Mrs. Sallie Glenn, 85, of Marion Route 1.

Mrs. Glenn, who was born the year that Effler was hanged, grew up hearing the story of the killing—from her mother's brother and sister, Uncle Joe Byrd and Aunt Ruth Byrd Burnette, who lived near the Efflers' house which was close to Buck Creek Gap; and from her husband, the late W.J. (Will) Glenn, who used to tell her about witnessing the hanging.

Will, 12, and his brother, Wash, 10, were taken by their father, David M. Glenn Sr., "to see Effler hung." According to Mrs. Glenn, "Will said he and Wash were standing up in the wagon bed so they could see, and when they were ready to cut the rope Wash lay down and put his head on his arms in the bottom of the bed and would not look. Will said Steve Effler had on a white vest (jacket) that looked like flax."

Bynum G. Finley of Marion, who is 87, has the old jail book kept by his father, A.L. (Fate) Finley, who was jailer from 1879 for a couple of terms under Sheriff Joe Neal.

The notation about Effler in the old pail [sic] book is a terse one:
"Steve Effler committed to jail 12th January 1881. Released 19th May 1882. Hung."

Bynum Finley remembers talks about the hanging. "Sheriff Neal and two deputies came up to my daddy that morning and said, 'Fate, we've got a job to do today....We've got to hang Effler.' My daddy said 'Ain't no we in this. You're the sheriff.' So the sheriff went down to Dysartsville and got a fellow named Landis to do the hanging."

The execution was carried out on a scaffold erected where the Drexel plant is now, close to a branch that came out of a hill, according to Bynum Finley.

And such a crowd came out to see it that "they said it looked like John Robinson's Circus," Finley heard his daddy say.

From time to time, somebody from the present generation has written a tale about the murder and colored it with a legend of how a justice of the peace, who had dreamed of being appealed to by a woman in distress, discovered that Peggy Grindstaff Effler had been done in by her husband.

MRS. GLENN'S ACCOUNT

To set the record straight, Mrs. Glenn has written the following story from the details she heard from her relatives.

"Steve Effler lived near the Buck Creek Gap on the McDowell County side. Ed Sowers lived on top of the mountain in Yancey County. Ed had stopped and talked with the Efflers as he passed on his way home. Steve and Peggy was having some disagreement about Peggy wanting to go home to see her folks at Red Hill.

"After Ed left going up the mountain, he heard Peggy screaming; that was late in the afternoon. On the Yancey County side, the snow was yet on the ground and crusted. About midnight that night, Ed heard someone walking in the snow, looked out, saw it was Steve Effler and thought of having heard that screaming.

"It wasn't long until Steve and his mother, Polly Effler, came by and asked Ed to go with them, that Peggy was very sick. As they went down the mountain Ed told Steve 'we can go faster than your mother,' so they ran on. Before they got there, they passed where some hogs were sleeping in an old shed. The hogs made a noise like groans, and Steve grabbed Ed and said, 'what was that?', and he was shaking.

"When they get to the door Steve made no attempt to go in, but began to call Peggy. Ed went right in, and while he was trying to get a light Steve went to the bed and began to lament and hollow, 'Peggy is dead.'

"Their baby boy, about two years old, was in bed asleep with his mother's dead body.

"A man was spending the night at Steve's father's and had heard them talking. Steve said he wanted his mother to go home with him, that Peggy had a fit and fell out of bed and he was afraid she was badly hurt. One of the women said, 'Steve, you have killed Peggy.' Peggy was a few months pregnant. That was all done away with; her clothes changed and floor and clothes washed. Steve had done all that before he went after his mother.

"Ed could see the floor had been washed, and some clothes. The neighbors of Job Effler, who lived near the head of South Toe River in Yancey County, came in (to the Steve Effler's). Elza Burnette and his wife Ruth—Aunt Ruth—said Peggy had some clothes packed around her neck and that she went to taking them off. Steve's mother Polly told her not to do that, that Peggy had such a pain in her head that her head would not lay straight.

"Ruth waited until she had a chance to move them—and Peggy's head rolled to one side. Ruth put the clothes back and went to where the men were making the coffin, and told them something was bad wrong. Elza Burnette rode his mule to Josh Young's in Yancey County, Josh being a J.P., and they went to J.R. Patton's and there they all decided what to do, knowing they would come by there taking Peggy's body to Red Hill to bury her. They deputized Jim Westall, and he stopped them and arrested Steve and they took the body in Patton's home and had an inquest. The crime being in McDowell County, they had a doctor from Marion—Dr. Virgil Butt Sr., a young man at that time. He quickly showed that Peggy's neck was broken, also her nose.

"Joe Neal was the sheriff at that time, 1881. After all the witnesses told what they knew—and the doctor—Steve confessed and said he took a piece of domestic cloth, put it around Peggy's neck, put his knee in back and pulled until her neck broke.

"Jim Westall kept close guard on him and kept one hand in his pocket all the time, Steve and Jim had grown up together and Jim said he knew how far Steve could run. He said, 'Steve, I know you can run like a deer; as sure as you do, I will kill you.' Steve said, 'I know I am going to be killed, but Jim I don't want you to do it.' They said Steve sat there looking like a wild, scared animal. All the time Jim didn't have anything in his pocket but a knife.

"After Steve confessed, he acted terrified as if some unseen demon was near him. Some of the witnesses were outside and they said they saw the devil himself, that he was as large as a mule, black as midnight, and about ten feet above the ground, in the air and shaking. Next morning there was no sign of tracks in the snow—all was smooth."

As a postscript to the story of the murder, Mrs. Glenn added that Peggy and Steve Effler's small son was reared by Steve's mother, Polly Effler. Mrs. Glenn's grandfather, David Byrd, who was born in 1815, used to tell her: "Polly Effler was a good woman. In the days when they had their fields all fenced with rails and cattle and hogs ran at large, they had a forest fire and it looked like all they had would be burnt. Men and women were working to get the fire checked. Grandfather said he came on top of a ridge and there was Polly on her knees, hands reaching toward heaven, and crying to the Lord to send rain. He said it was not hours, it was then, while she was yet on her knees, that the rain came and he never saw in his life more rain; it poured and put out all the fire."

THE COURT RECORD

While the actual evidence presented in a trial isn't recorded in the court minutes, much is told in the court records about the Effler case. The bill of indictment returned against Effler at the spring term of 1881, which opened the 28th day of March with Judge Allmand A. McCoy presiding and Solicitor Joseph S. Adams prosecuting for the state, is lengthy and brutally descriptive:

"The grand jurors come into court and present the following bills of indictment, to wit: State against Stephan Effler, indictment murder:

"The jurors for the state upon their oath present that Stephen Effler, late of the county of McDowell, laborer, not having the fear of God before his eyes, but being moved and seduced by the instigation of the Devil, on the sixth day of January in the year of our Lord 1881, with force and arms, at and in the county aforesaid, in and upon one Peggie Effler in the peace of Goda nd the State then and there being feloniously, willfully and of his malice aforethought did strike, beat, kick and choke the said Peggie Effler with both his hands and feet in and upon the head, nose, neck, side and other parts of the body of her the said Peggie Effler...and did cast and throw the said Peggie Effler down, upon and unto the ground with great violence, then giving...several mortal bruises, and fractures in and upon the head, nose, neck and sides, and breaking the neck of the said Peggie...(who) then and there instantly died." The description goes further, recording the size of the various "Mortal wounds" and ends by alleging that Stephen "did wilfully and of malice aforethought did kill and murder...."

Among the 10 prosecuting witnesses listed in the court record are Mrs. Glenn's relatives, "Ells Burnett, Ruth Burnett."

Effler went on trial at the fall term of 1881, the court using up members of a special venire of 60 jurors and then summoning 50 others. Effler was found guilty and sentenced to hang on "Friday the 11th day of November, 1881, on which day between the hours of eleven and two o'clock he shall be taken to the place of execution appointed by law and there be hanged by the neck until he be dead."

Attorneys for Effler appealed. The Supreme Court's finding of "no error in the trial and conviction" appears in the local court minutes for the spring term of 1882. Defense counselors then argued that Effler "has become insane since his trial and conviction," so the court ordered a jury to be sworn and impaneled to try the question of the prisoner's insanity or sanity. The jury's verdict: Effler is not insane.

And now the final judgment is entered: That on Friday, May 19, 1882, between 11 and 2 o'clock Effler be hanged "by the neck until he be dead. May the Lord have mercy upon his soul."

[Note: John Harden established the first public relations firm in North
Carolina. He was also active in the successful political campaigns of several
North Carolina governors. Throughout his life, he collected stories and
legends from all parts of the state. He had a radio program and published
numerous newspaper and magazine articles on North Carolina folklore. In
addition to this book, he also published *The Devil's Tramping Ground*, another
collection of superstitions and stories. It's anybody's guess as to why he felt
compelled to change the names in the Stephen Effler murder story. It illus-
trates how each storyteller adds to the story every time it is told.]

But for a dream the perfect crime might have been committed in McDowell
County back in the 1870s. Stalking in ghostly fashion through the misty world
of dreams, a stranger was selected, in this instance, to bring justice to the North
Carolina hill country.

A young farmer named George Feller lived in the Buck Creek Gap section of
McDowell County in 1879, with his wife, Kathy, and an infant son. He had a
hard struggle to keep things going. Farming in the Blue Ridge Mountains is
not easy, and Mrs. Feller suffered from chronic asthma, to the point that she
was a semi-invalid and could do but a few of the things traditionally required
of a farmer's wife.

Early one morning Feller knocked at a neighbor's door and, amid sobs,
asked for help. He said his wife was taken with an attack more violent than
usual and that he was fearful she would die. The matter of a doctor meant
hours of time and miles on horseback. He said he was at his wits' end in
seeking to help Kathy gain relief or any degree of comfort.

The sympathetic friends responded quickly. But when they arrived at the
Feller cabin they found the young wife dead in her bed, the baby sleeping
beside her still-warm body. Feller wept uncontrollably. The kind mountain
people took over with their usual neighborliness. Plans were made to meet the
immediate shock, and for the funeral and burial that were to follow.

The men assembled, made a coffin of rough boards, and dug a grave in the bosom of the mountain. The women prepared the body. Kathy was dressed and "laid out," in keeping with the custom of the day.

Word of the death spread throughout the community and stolid-faced neighbors called by to indicate their concern, in halting voices. A special messenger made the ten-mile trip to Mrs. Feller's original home to notify relatives there. The community preacher brought consolation to the saddened home and remained for hours to add the comfort and faith he felt were needed.

At the funeral home a motley procession formed. The coffin was placed in the bed of a two-horse wagon for its slow journey along the difficult course to the cemetery, four miles away. The mourners walked sadly behind.

When little more than two miles along the way the procession met a middle-aged man astride a horse. He blocked the narrow roadway and signaled the driver of the wagon to a halt. No one knew or recognized the stranger. As he spoke the little knot of mountain people listened in silent horror.

"You can't bury this woman," the stranger said. "She has been murdered!"

The mourning husband, sitting beside the driver of the wagon, with his baby in his lap, stared blankly into space. Some of the men around him flushed up angrily at the stranger's intrusion and accusation. Astonishment was general.

"I don't know any of you," the stranger continued. "I live over in Yancey County. But I dreamed last night that on my way into McDowell I would meet a funeral procession with a coffin containing the body of a woman who had been killed by her husband. This is just the group I saw in my sleep, the same wagon, the same coffin. Unless you have an examination made I am going to report this whole thing to the law."

The man was convincing in his talk; he seemed honest and sincere. Feller's neighbors gathered in a knot to talk things over in subdued voices.

These natives of the southern mountain country believed implicitly in dreams. They thought that each dream had a meaning, and that if dreams could be interpreted they carried messages from another world. However, the neighbors were inclined to disregard the stranger—until one of them pointed to the significant fact that, although he was a stranger, the man knew that the coffin contained the body of a young woman.

Agreeing that the whole thing was ridiculous, the group of mountain neighbors concluded that there would be some merit in having a doctor look at the woman before she was buried, since she had been unattended in death. In view of the unfathomable dream of the convincing stranger, anything else would leave unanswered questions, veiled accusations, and a great deal of "talk" in the mountain community for years to come.

So, with mild objections from George Feller, the cortege turned its course from the cemetery to Marion, the county seat, where a man of medicine was available. "The thing to do," but "silly," they said to each other all the way to town.

However, the doctor who examined the body didn't think so. He said Kathy Feller had died of strangulation all right, but strangulation caused by pressure on the *outside* of her neck rather than by an asthmatic condition. There was evidence, he said, that the pressure had been smooth and even over a wide area of the throat and not concentrated enough to make noticeable bruises. Because of her ailment, less pressure was needed to stop Kathy's breathing than would have been the case with a person not suffering from her particular ailment.

The mountain people looked at each other and at George Feller. The women could recall nothing amiss during burial preparations. The men recalled George's tears.

George Feller began to fidget. His eyes wouldn't look straight at the neighbors as they tried to talk to him, but shifted about and fixed themselves first on his hands and then on the floor. The doctor sent for the sheriff.

What Feller did say began to conflict and get more and more confused. The sheriff told the little knot of people to take Feller's baby and go home, that he would hold the young mountaineer there until things could be straightened out. Placing Feller in jail, the sheriff drove his buggy around to the home of the justice of the peace and the two of them went out to the Feller cabin in the hills. They searched the house carefully to see what light might be shed on the strange case.

Finally light came, like a beam from the summer sun, out of a homemade chest in the sleeping section of the two-room log house. There they found a broad band of rawhide that looked as if it might have been used as a garrote. Closer examination revealed a few long golden hairs, just like Kathy Feller's, still clinging to the rough edges of the greenish leather.

They took the band to the jail. When the sheriff walked into Feller's cell with it in his hand, George collapsed and told what had happened.

He and Kathy had a big fuss, he said. It went on way into the night, getting more and more violent. Finally in an insane rage he put the leather strap around the neck of his sick and weakened wife and held it tightly with his powerful hands until she collapsed on the bed. Realizing what he had done, but reasoning that neighbors who had seen Kathy struggle for breath would easily believe that his wife's bronchial complaint had finally choked her to death, he decided on that deception.

And the cruel murderer played the role of the sorrowing husband in a way to carry conviction. He was even able to win the further sympathy of neighbors.

At his trial George Feller confessed everything. He was sentenced to death on the gallows. His execution was the last hanging staged in McDowell County.

And a weird piece of justice was added as a sort of final flourish to the last chapter of George Feller's crime and punishment. The drop from the gallows did not break the neck of the murderer. *He died of strangulation!*

5. Monroe Thomas' Account

[Author's Note: Although I never had the privilege of meeting the man, Monroe Thomas remains a personal hero of mine. The following article about him by a cousin explains why. Although severely crippled, Thomas turned out hundreds of pages on the history of families in Mitchell and Yancey Counties. In careful, no doubt painful fashion, he carefully wrote all this out by hand. It took him two hours to transcribe a single page of lined notebook paper. He was an intellectual giant among the mountain people and his influence is still profoundly felt in our area, not least of all by the author of this book. The following article was written by Thomas' cousin, John Silver Harris of Boca Raton, Florida, and published in Volume I of Lloyd Bailey's Heritage of the Toe River Valley. It is reprinted here by permission.]

Monroe Thomas (1903-1957) of Kona was a remarkable man. He suffered from osteomyelitis, an inflammatory bone and muscle-wasting disease. Despite his affliction, he attended Yancey Collegiate Institute at Burnsville, qualified as a teacher, and taught five or six years at Kona, Crabtree, Hawk and Altapass.

By 1939, his malady had so crippled him he could no longer teach, forcing him to return home to spend his remaining 18 years as an invalid. But while osteomyelitis crippled his body, his sharp mind was unfettered. He read widely in many academic fields—literature, philosophy, history, psychology, religion, mathematics, and the sciences.

In spite of his afflictions, he actively pursued his intellectual interests, keeping up with the outside world through books sent by the state library system and through correspondence and visits from other scholars in the region. His reading furnished him with good models for writing and he was a keen observer of life around him.

During his short lifetime (he died at 53 in 1957), he filled several volumes with observations on the life, people and public concerns around him. He also wrote poetry and short stories which reflect the mountain culture. Using his left hand, which was not crippled, he filled notebook after notebook with neat, distinctive script.

Thomas was included in a June, 1958 National Geographic article (with photograph) entitled, "My Neighbors Hold to Mountain Ways," in which he is called "a backwood saint." [The magazine also printed a photograph of Thomas' poem, "Contentment," an amazing realization of a mental state of peace and calm by one so horribly afflicted.]

Thomas was also the subject of a play, entitled "The Gentle Giant of Kona," presented in 1986 at Mountain Heritage School in Burnsville, N.C. "Monroe Thomas deserves the name of 'giant' not because of his physical stature but because of the strength of his mind and will," said a spokesman for the Toe River Arts Council, the play's sponsor.

[Author's note: The following story is published with permission of Dr. Jo Ann Thomas (Mrs. Richard) Croom of Mars Hill, N.C., who inherited the papers of her beloved uncle, Monroe Thomas. Thomas went to a great deal of trouble to get his handwritten manuscript typed by a woman in Spruce Pine named Mrs. Rom Duncan. She reluctantly charged him $4.50. Thomas wrote the article and hoped to see it published in the Saturday Evening Post. The magazine obviously rejected the piece, but a letter of rejection was not found among Thomas' papers.]

THE STEPHEN EFFLER MURDER CASE

Behold, the wicked man conceives evil
    and is pregnant with mischief,
    and brings forth lies.
He makes a pit, digging it out,
    and falls into the hole which he has made.
His mischief returns upon his own head,
    and on his own pate his violence descends.
        —King David

By

Monroe Thomas

Kona Rural Station
Bakersville, North Carolina
December, 1955

THE STEPHEN EFFLER MURDER CASE

That a man slew his young wife in the dead of night and put out a report that she had died a natural death; that he was the next day unexpectedly halted on his way to the cemetery and arrested as the suspected slayer; that he later confessed to the crime, and was tried, convicted, and hanged; and that the only suspicion which led to his arrest and confession was a dream dreamed by a man in another community forms as weird and stirring a tale as any ever carried by a detective mystery. Yet that is what once actually happened here in the mountains of western North Carolina.

The time was 1881—the year that Old Mother Shipton predicted that this old world to an end would come—the place was the little community of Buck Creek Gap in McDowell County, North Carolina, and the slayer was Stephen Effler, scion of a prominent pioneer family. The time, the place, and the slayer were happily met. In those days in that place a man was his own doctor, and death certificates were unheard of; when death entered a man's home his neighbors came in and put his dead out of sight and asked questions only to weep with him. Effler chose a dark autumn night to slay his comely young wife by strangulation, and removed every trace of evidence that might lead to a suspicion of his crime, then putting out a report that she had died a natural death, he made arrangements for the funeral and was on his way to the cemetery when a man from another community chanced to meet him and ordered the funeral procession to halt for a post-mortem examination of the corpse.

The man's action was as daring as it was unexpected, and the only reason that he had for it was a dream that he had dreamed the night before; he had no other evidence or suspicion and had not even heard of the woman's death until he chanced to meet the funeral procession on its way to the cemetery. But in the inquest which followed, the real cause of the woman's death was discovered and the husband was arrested on the spot as the suspected slayer and taken to jail. In the silence of jail he confessed to the crime, and was tried, convicted, and hanged—all because the man who dreamed the dream chance to meet him at the opportune moment and had the courage and conviction to act.

The solution of this slaying was one of the weirdest, most dramatic events that ever took place in our Southern Mountains and perhaps in the whole of American criminology. Bold, unexpected, and unheard of, it was filled from beginning to end with a high element of the supernatural and moved with climactic swiftness; from the unexpected halting of the funeral procession on its way to the cemetery to the fulfilling of the last grim prediction of the condemned man on the scaffold of execution it held the whole countryside gripped in the suspense of high drama; and it is still avidly read and discussed by a mystery-loving public.

But as with all great stories it has many variations. The following version, told to the writer by the late Reverend Jimmy Thomas, of Newdale, and James Hutchins, of Burnsville, Route 2, gives the story, for the first time, in full in writing, and is an eyewitness account. A young man at the time, the Reverend Thomas was personally acquainted with the slayer and his wife and the man who dreamed the dream and witnessed both the autopsy and the hanging; and Mr. Hutchins, a former Superintendent of Education of Yancey County, grew up not many years later in a near-by community and had the story from many authentic sources.

The little community of Buck Creek Gap lies on the crest of the Blue Ridge Mountains, and is partly in McDowell County and partly in Yancey. At that time it was a pioneer crossroads community between two drainage systems and two ways of life, but with the coming of motor-accessible highways its lofty position and panoramic view under the evening shadow of Mt. Mitchell gave it the added attraction of scenic grandeur and converted it into one of the wonder spots of the Southern Highlands. Locally, however, it still derives its chief importance from the fact that it is one of the main southern gateways to fruitful and mineral-rich Toe River Valley, the high, narrow mountain valley curving northward from the Grandfather Mountain area around by Mt. Mitchell to the Roan and composed politically of the three counties of Mitchell, Avery and Yancey, a Republican stronghold known collectively as Mayland.

The Efflers lived just over the crest of the mountains on the McDowell side of Buck Creek Gap, near the place where the Scenic Parkway now intersects the Marion-to-Micaville highway. Effler was a native of the region, but his wife was from the Snow Creek Community of Mitchell County on the Toe River Valley side of the mountains. She was Peggy Grindstaff, daughter of Joe Grindstaff, to whose home Effler had gone only a few years before to court and marry her.

A handsome, wiry young farmer and homeworker, Effler was well brought up, intelligent, quick-witted, and possessed of strong passions and great personal daring. As a child he had been marked by a tendency to extreme cruelty, but through the vigorous discipline of his parents he had overcome the worst of his childhood savageries as he grew up, and was not markedly different from his neighbors. It was known that the flow of warm blood affected him strangely, causing in him a wild gladness over which he seemingly had no control, and that he lacked feeling and was contemptuous of the sufferings of others; but nobody paid any attention to these things, and if he had ever been cruel to Peggy no one had any knowledge of it. In fact, the impression that people got of his relationship to her was the exact opposite of cruelty; she was the one person in the world whom he seemed to regard with genuine tenderness.

In the fall of 1881, times were hard in the mountains of Western North Carolina, the economic disruptions caused by the Civil War not yet having been overcome, and the Effler homestead found itself in financial straits. The only solution was for Effler to seek work elsewhere, and accordingly he left the home in charge of Peggy and took his departure, ending up in near-by Madison County, where he found employment in the harvest fields. Most of that fall he spent out there, returning at infrequent intervals to visit Peggy and their infant son.

It was during his stay in Madison County that his affections for Peggy began to wane. The cause was a love affair which sprang up between him and a woman who lived near the place of his employment. One day as he labored in the fields and mused on the changed state of his heart, the thought came to him, and persisted, that except for Peggy he would be free to marry this other woman; and from that day forward he began to devise means whereby he might free himself from her without jeopardizing his own name and position.

The idea of secretly killing his wife and pretending that she had died a natural death came to him one autumn evening as he journeyed home on one of his infrequent visits. The idea appealed to him as the safest and quickest way that he had yet thought of for ridding himself of her, and he hurriedly decided in favor of it; and so great was his impatience to get it over and done with and return to Madison a free man that he resolved to carry it out that very night and set to work to formulate his plans as he journeyed along, becoming so absorbed in them that he hardly noticed the passing distance at all. Sooner or later there comes a time in every man's life when a man has to take things into his own hands, he reasoned; but his main concern was how to ward off all suspicion from himself, and to better effect that purpose he stopped at his nearest neighborhood store and noisily bought his wife a new pair of store shoes, the gift par excellence in those days. A little surprise for the finest wife a man ever had, he boasted to the wide-eyed onlookers—and knew that his plus his wife's known seizures of a violent pain in her head was all he needed to effect his purpose.

A glad surprise, indeed, the shoes would have been for Peggy had not another surprise of a different sort awaited her. For, acting according to plan, Effler refused to share as usual their common bed that night. He spread a pallet on the hearth before the fire and proposed to sleep on it, using as a pretext the excuse that he was travel-sore and weary and wanted to be alone. Peggy was no doubt used to his whims, but nevertheless we can imagine that in the face of this strange behavior she forgot all about the shoes and went to bed disturbed and saddened and lay a long time wakeful, feeling alone and forsaken.

Effler also lay down, but not to sleep; fully girded and shod, he tossed fitfully on his pallet before the fire and counted off the minutes as they ticked away to the appointed hour. Finally, in the still watches of midnight silences, the hour arrived, and he sat up and listened. The low-smouldering fire flickered and fretted, but other than this the only sound was the deep rhythm of Peggy's sleeping, and that was the sound he wanted to hear. By the pale half-light of the fire he arose and made his way to the far corner of the room, where he unwound from the beam of the loom a narrow band of newly woven domestic cloth which he knew was there. Then slipping noiselessly to the bed of his sleeping wife, he slowly eased down the pillow beneath her neck and inserted one end of the cloth through the opening thus formed; then drawing the two ends together to form a loop around her neck he started twisting—the longer the harder and the more furiously.

When all struggle had ended he let the cloth fall slack and waited. There was no more movement. His whole being throbbed with a wild exultation, and he wanted to jump up and down and shout; but he remembered that he had a far different role to play and little time to lose, and this had a sobering effect on him. He removed the cloth and put it back where it belonged, then took up his pallet and tidied up the bed with its still form, being careful to make it look as if he had just got up from his place on the other side. Then properly disarraying his clothes to indicate hurried dressing, he went tearing off to the home of one of his neighbors and roused them up. He was all out of breath and greatly agitated. Would they get up and come quick? Peggy was bad-off. All evening she had complained that she could taste blood, and a little while ago she had waked him up, ravin' distracted and cryin', "My head! My head!" He reckoned she'd had another seizure of her old pain; it was the worst spell he'd ever seen her have, and if something wasn't done quick hit'd be too late. But he didn't know what to do. She was speechless when he left., and he was afraid she was dying and might even then be dead. Alarmed, the family hastily arose and returned with him, only to find her as he had feared—dead.

News of the death spread rapidly and by daybreak most of the neighbors knew about it and had come in to offer their services and sympathy. Effler acted his part well and was the very picture of suffering, sorrowing grief. He told repeatedly how his wife had waked him in the night, and how in hopeless desperation he had gone for help; and he made much of the fact that she had died alone. But what was a man to do? Was he to stand idly by while his wife died and not try to do something to save her? Life was made up of many ingredients and one had to take the bitter with the sweet. He got out the pair of shoes and tried to tell their story, but emotion got the better of him and, weeping copiously, he set them away. Everyone present was visibly affected, and no one, not even those who dressed his wife and laid her out, saw anything that wasn't explainable by the known facts. We all have to die, and it was just another death.

It was decided to take her back to her girlhood home in Mitchell County for burial, and with the coming of dawn a swift messenger on horseback was dispatched to carry the sad news back there and get the grave ready. Effler was to follow at a more leisurely pace with the corpse, and as the journey by slow-moving wagon would take most of the day, it was decided to start with as little delay as possible in order to get there in time for the burial late that evening. Accordingly, a casket was hastily procured and the body was placed in it. Then those friends and neighbors who planned to accompany Effler as mourners gathered, and the funeral procession formed and started on its long and sorrowful journey—a journey that in all likelihood would have ended well for Effler had not a certain unexpected circumstance lay across his path which no man in his situation could have foreseen.

To acquaint ourselves in advance with that strange circumstance let us hasten on ahead of Effler and his unsuspecting fellow-travelers. We will let them overtake us presently at the opportune time.

Effler was not the only one who had tossed restlessly on his bed the night before and counted off the hours as they droned away toward the midnight silences. A certain man in a neighboring community had retired early that night but slept only briefly, then waked and tossed restlessly, seeking sleep that would not return. That man was Joshua Young, a prosperous middle-aged farmer of the Browns Creek section of South Toe River. But it was not concern for the Efflers that had kept him awake. He lived five miles or more below the Efflers on the Yancey side of Buck Creek Gap, and although he knew them when he saw them he was not closely or intimately acquainted with them. Living in a separate community, he attended a different church from theirs and went to a different store and mill, and consequently he saw them only occasionally and had no social or business relations with them. If he had ever spoken more than a word in passing to either of them he had no remembrance of it.

The Efflers therefore never once consciously crossed his mind as he tossed on his bed that night. It was something else that occasioned his unrest: a vague, undefinable inner disquiet that he could never quite center his thoughts on. A long time he tossed, but in the still watches of the midnight hours he finally dozed off—and dreamed a most disquieting dream: a young woman in great distress, whom he knew but could not place, suddenly stood before him, and showing him her bruised neck, cried that she was being murdered and implored him to avenge her death. The dream ended abruptly and he awoke, troubled to the depth of his soul. As he pondered on what the dream could mean and tried to think who the young woman was, he suddenly dozed off again and dreamed the same dream a second time in all its disturbing vivid-ness. Then he awoke and slept no more that night.

If Joshua Young had that power which is today termed psychic he was not aware of it. Neither was he a mystic or a religious fanatic. Like many others around him, and like many still found in the Toe River Valley section of our Southern Highlands—a region, by the way, which Toynbee is pleased to describe as "worse than barbarian"—he was brought up to read the Bible, and walked in the knowledge and fear of the Lord. But he was not given to dreaming dreams and seeing visions. He was a deeply rugged, resolute man who had lived and prospered by the labor of his hands, and though kindly and devout he was a man of few words and the possessor of an indomitable will and courage. When he spoke people sat up and listened.

Nevertheless Joshua Young was deeply troubled in his mind and spirit that morning. He tried to put the dream out of his thoughts, but the agonized face of the young woman refused to leave. He was troubled by the strange way in which she eluded his recognition, ever coming within his grasp and ever fleeing; and he was troubled most of all by the fact that she had stood before him in the same agony of distress a second time. Thinking silence the best way to forget, he made no mention of his dream to his family, and after a hasty breakfast hurried out to his work, hoping to find forgetfulness in labor. But the longer he worked the more troubled he became. Finally, he could endure the torture of it no longer, and laying down the tools of his employment he decided to go over and unbosom himself to his friend and neighbor John Patton and seek comfort and an explanation from him.

Patton lived two miles over the way on the Marion-to-Micaville road, only Micaville was then called Big Crabtree. Patton was an officer of the law and empowered to write injunctions, make arrests and do all the other acts necessary to maintaining the peace and order of the community. But that fact never entered Young's mind as he trudged along, for it is only the violators of the law who are conscious of the law's embodiment. Young had no thought for anything but his dream; behind its veiled mystery, he believed, lay a hidden meaning, and if anybody could help him to solve that mystery and find its meaning it was his friend and neighbor John Patton.

He found Patton at home. The two men went into Patton's private study, the front windows of which gave a view of the road, and closed and bolted the door. For Young was fearful lest his dream be overheard and fall into the hands of the local interpreters; he could already envisage the kind of construction they'd put on it, and how, if they got hold of it, it'd be the talk of every home in the community before nightfall. Thus secured, the guest began his story. He had barely finished when they looked up and saw a procession, evidently of mourners, slowly winding into view up the road. What did that mean? They hadn't heard of any death up the way. Without further discussion, they got up, unfastened the door and went out to see what it did mean.

The procession slowly moved up alongside of the two men and stopped. It was Effler and his neighbors from Buck Creek Gap on their way to the distant cemetery in Mitchell County—some in wagons, some on horseback, and some afoot. Greetings were exchanged, and the two men, seeing the casket in the wagon beside Effler, anxiously inquired who was dead. Hadn't they heard?

Effler asked, surprised—and once again told his story. The two men in turn expressed surprise and extended their sympathy, and Effler observed that the morning was coming on apace and they had a long hard journey before them. Then picking up the lines, he was about to drive on, but suddenly, as if struck by an afterthought, he let them drop again. Were the men acquainted with his wife? Without waiting for a reply, he put the lines aside and, slipping back the lid of the casket, magnanimously invited them to stop up and take a last look at the dear departed face before he drove on.

Patton stepped up and looked, and then stepped aside to make room for his companion. Young then stepped up and looked—and when he did so it seemed as if an unseen hand suddenly reached out and gripped him by the throat and held him tight. The face in the casket was the face of the young woman in his dream! Overwhelmed by the sudden and unexpected revelation, he wrenched himself loose and reeled back as if he had been struck and stood appalled, pale and trembling. But his confusion was only for a moment and those who stood by thought he had suddenly been overcome by grief; they could not know that during that brief moment he had passed through a great emotional upheaval and made an equally momentous decision.

At this point it would be in style to say something grandly moving and dramatic about Joshua Young's consciousness of himself as an instrument of Heaven, only such a consciousness did not exist. From the beginning he had been troubled by the feeling that because his dream had been given to him a second time it had been given for a purpose, but it was not until afterwards that he realized that he had been the instrument of Heaven and supernaturally guided and sustained. The thing that moved him now was his recognition of the face in the casket as the face of the young woman in his dream; he now knew who it was that had stood before him in the agony of death the night before and cried for help—and knowing this made all the difference in the world. It was Peggy Effler! Recognition had come with the swiftness of a lightning stroke the moment he had looked into the casket, and with the same overpowering swiftness the meaning of his dream had cleared and his duty, bare and resplendent, had arisen out of the welter of his mind and stood beckoning him on, albeit against stupendous odds.

For Joshua Young was not now one groping blindly in the dark for a clue to a mystery that he did not understand; he was a man transformed—confident, sure, and supremely aware of the decisive importance of the moment. The time, however, had been so brief as to be almost instantaneous, and as no word had yet been spoken those who stood by had no way of knowing that the whole complexity of the situation before him, and of his relationship to it, had suddenly changed. They had no way of knowing that the deathly pallor of his face was caused, not by tears restrained, as they supposed, but by the wild deliriousness that suddenly intoxicates one who rises out of struggle triumphant and sees his duty invitingly beckoning him on; or that the trembling of his hands was caused, not by emotional weakness, but by the awful fear that this moment would somehow slip out of his grasp unused and the opportunity for doing what he had to do would forever be lost.

For although Joshua Young was not a man given to acting on the impulse of the moment, yet time was of the very essence of his plan. Turning to Effler, he asked him as casually as he could if he'd wait a little longer till he and Patton could go into the house and return. This was the first word that had been spoken since Effler had invited the two men to look into the casket, and thinking that he'd scored an important victory and Young wanted to fetch flowers, Effler readily consented, and the two men went up the worn rock laid path and entered the house. Once inside, Young hurriedly told Patton of his discovery and, violating the belief that his dream was a trust laid upon him, asked for the legal authority to act, lest the opportune moment pass and the agonized plea of that innocent young face torture him for the rest of his days.

The authority granted, the two men returned, and Young told his dream and gave an outline of the circumstances that led him up to his recognition of the face in the casket as the face of the young woman who had stood before him and cried for help. For as much as he recoiled at the thought of making his dream public he hated false pretense more, and since he had to give a cause for his action he deemed it unthinkable to give any but the true one, and so he omitted nothing but boldly told everything. Then in a voice deep with solemnity but vibrant with mounting tension, he offered it as his opinion that inasmuch as the dream had been given to him twice it had been given for a purpose—and in the name of the law commanded the funeral procession to halt, and to remain halted, until the true cause of the young woman's death could be determined.

It was the funeral party's turn now to reel back overwhelmed and stand appalled, stunned and speechless. If a bomb had unexpectedly been exploded in their midst it would not have caused greater consternation. Everyone stood with mouth open, speechless and dumbfounded. Yet, strangely enough, it was Effler, upon whom the awful implications fell but who alone was in the possession of the facts, who recovered first. The others had not known what to expect until the bolt fell, but almost from the first word Effler had sensed what was coming and was in a measure prepared for it.

His first reaction was to treat it as a colossal joke; slapping his thighs and laughing uproariously, he cried for the next one who had eaten too many boiled cabbage for supper the night before to step forward and tell his dream—and started whipping up his horses to get going. But before he could get under way he felt the chilling hands of the law's embodiment enclosing on the lines about his own and taking them out of his grasp. Drawing the horses back till their traces hung loose, Patton tied the lines fast to the wagon and ordered him to leave them tied there until he was bidden by the proper authorities to untie them and drive on.

It was then that the awful predicament into which he had stumbled began to sink in upon Effler. He had expected the annoying questions and pryings of his neighbors, and it was this that had carried him through the initial shock; but he had not expected such an encounter as this, and he was utterly unprepared for it. The supernatural aspects of his situation probably escaped him altogether, but nonetheless heknew that he was trapped, and the realization bewildered and frightened him. What did these men know, and what were they up to? Where had they been snooping around the night before? They had somehow got wind of what he had done, he believed, and the dream was only a ruse to draw him out and make him witness against himself. Yet the more he tried to think the more bewildered and alarmed he became. He was seized with a wild impulse to flee, but restrained it as the one sure way to proclaim his guilt; and he felt terror and rage taking possession of him, but he choked them back and tried persuasion seasoned with bluff instead.

What they were doing, he said, was a dangerous thing; it was no less than an accusation against himself—and he protested his innocence and called high heaven and earth as witness. Having found his tongue, he put up a good argument in his behalf and begged to be believed and allowed to continue his sorrow-laden journey. It was not of himself that he was thinking, he cried; he had nothing to fear. His concern was for the corpse and the waiting loved ones. The morning was all but gone, and in that sun who could say how much longer before a stench would start. That was the cause of his seeming alarm and eagerness to get going. If his detainers would put themselves in his place they'd understand better the seriousness of what they were doing, and instead of hindering would be hastening him along.

The others of the party, having by now somewhat recovered from their initial shock, joined him in his plea and pointed out that if violence had been done surely some evidence of it would have remained. Yet there was none. The house had been in order, the room and bed in which the woman lay was in order, and the woman who bathed and dressed her and laid her out had found nothing amiss. There was not even a suggestion of violence, and it had not occurred to them to doubt Effler's story. As for the dream, everybody had those troubled, distorted visions of the nighttime; they came on the wings of the night and left on the wings of the night, but what caused them or what they portended was more than any man could say.

To all of which Young made answer. There was nothing personal in his action, he said, and it was not meant as an accusation against Effler. He had barely known Effler and had known his wife only when he saw her, and although his action might seem to belie his words, it was not doubt of Effler's story that was driving him on; it was the agonized cry of the young woman whose face and voice never left him, and whom he now knew to be the young woman in the casket. For if it had been granted to them to see what he had seen they would not call it common, a vision of the nighttime that comes and goes and the moment thereafter is forgotten; nor would they think his action strange. It was a living force, without flesh and blood—yes, but nonetheless a living force, a thing of the spirit. At the opportune moment he had made the recognition, and having made it he could not do otherwise than he was doing. Tomorrow or next week would be too late; now was the time, and now it must be.

Effler's cup of anguish now filled to overflowing. He did not fear the outcome for his person. He was certain that he'd left no telltale marks on his wife's body, and he was equally certain that no court of law would convict him on the evidence of a dream. But full well he knew what it would do to his reputation and to his chances with the other woman. It would cast a shadow over his life that he'd be years in living down. Yet there was nothing now that he could do but hide his fears and rage as best he could and submit.

Accordingly, a messenger on horseback was dispatched at breakneck speed to Burnsville, the county seat of Yancey County, to get the coroner to come and make an examination of the corpse and settle the matter. At the same time other messengers, unbidden, sped north, east, south, and west, and by midafternoon when the first messenger returned with his man a great crowd had gathered and everyone was avidly seeking to discover from his neighbor what had happened and what it all meant. Things had come to a bad out, they 'low'd, when a man couldn't bury his own dead and get them out of his sight without being stopped on the big road by some dreamer of dreams and made to sign a death warrant; and if they did such things in broad daylight what would they do in the dark?

The coroner was a young man, a political appointee and without medical training. A hush of expectancy fell on the crowd when his presence became known, and he was led to the wagon where, grim and unspeaking, the three men waited by the casket. Having been acquainted with the nature of the case on the way, he asked for the facts concerning the woman's death. Effler told his story. Who had stopped him, and why? Effler pointed to Young. Young told his dream. Why else had he stopped him? The dream was not his only reasons, was it? Yes, the dream was his only reason. He opened the casket and looked at the face of the corpse. A pretty face, he remarked, then closed it and turned to Young. For a full minute he studied him up and down, then unexpectedly asked him if he knew what year and century it was. Young answered that it was the eighty-first year, of what he believed a large portion of mankind commonly referred to as the nineteenth century. He didn't know whether he knew or not, he said; his action was the most preposterous, the most unheard-of thing that he'd ever met with, and it made one think he was back in the Middle Ages. And laughing him to scorn, he turned to Effler and told him to untie his lines and drive on.

If Effler had done as bidden, he would no doubt have made his escape and been exonerated by society; and Young's humiliation and defeat would have been his revenge, and a sufficient one. But he didn't do this; he tarried to put out his wrath upon Young—and the second time that day brought about his own defeat. He had a quick tongue and was good at vituperation. He wanted to remind Young before he drove on, he said, that he had a little matter to settle with him. He'd like to settle it then and there, but he was on an errand of sorrow and could not settle it that day. But when he returned he'd settle it; he'd teach him that it didn't pay to dream about other men's wives. How he'd teach him was none of Young's business. Young had called the tunes on the first round, but now it was his turn to call them and he was going to see to it that he danced right merrily.

Young stood with bowed head and answered not a word, but it was not Effler's threats, as Effler and the crowd supposed, that had bowed and silenced him, but the awful fear that he had had in the beginning, the fear that this moment would somehow slip out of his hands unused. In his despair he scarcely heard a word of what Effler said; he was conscious only of the inadequacy of the examination. There was not a farmer in the whole country-side, he told himself over and over, who could not have done as much, and was this to be his answer to the young woman who, he now knew, lay cold and voiceless in the casket beside him? It could not be! It must not be!—but how could he keep it from being? Could he halt the funeral party a second time? And if so, on what grounds and to what purpose? There was no one above the coroner to whom he could appeal; in such matters his decision was final.

This was the problem that, with bowed head and in silence, Joshua Young grappled with as Effler poured out his threats; freed from restraints and sensing the sympathy of the crowd, Effler thrilled to the attack and laid it on heavy, but whether he actually meant to return and do what he threatened, or whether he had no intention of returning and could afford to be lavish, we shall never know. For toward the end of his philippic Young found a way out of his difficulties—and was astounded by what he found. For he now knew that the very foundation had been pulled from under them and whatever the coroner's decision might have been he would have had no choice but to oppose it. He let Effler finish, but before he could untie his lines and drive on he slowly straightened up and spread his hands abroad in the manner of a preacher asking for attention. Instantly there was a hush and every eye fastened itself upon him.

He spoke in the same solemn, tension-packed voice that he had used earlier in the day. They had made a mistake, he said, a very serious mistake. For they had been acting all the while on the assumption that the deceased was a citizen of Yancey County, whereas she was both a citizen of and had died in McDowell. What did that mean? He was speaking to men who knew the law and had regard for the right. Did it not mean that their whole day's work had thereby been rendered null and void, and that the examination to be lawful would have to be performed anew—performed by the proper officer of

McDowell County? Yes, that was exactly what it meant, he cried—and in the name of the law commanded the funeral party to halt, and to remain halted, until the true cause of the young woman's death could be lawfully determined.

Effler's distress at this unexpected turn in his affairs bordered on the ludicrous. He appealed first to the coroner and then to the crowd to save him, but the coroner waved him back and cried that if they wanted to fight it out over a dream to go to it and a plague on them both! And the crowd had just given their assent to Young and were in no mood to change. The coroner then made off as if he were leaving, but it is worthy of note that he soon returned by another route and remained to see how the matter ended; and the most that the crowd would do was to grudgingly assure Effler that if he had done no evil he had nothing to fear from the law, that on the contrary the law would be his best friend. Seeing all hope of intervention vanish, Effler then fell back on his old plea for sympathy, crying that it was not of himself but of the state of the corpse that he was thinking, but as his wife by his own count had been dead only a little over twelve hours this got him nowhere, and once more the messenger rode forth at breakneck speed, this time over the mountains to Marion, county seat of McDowell County, and with Young's express orders to fetch a doctor.

And once more the messengers unbidden sped out on the four winds and the people poured in. If the surrounding hills and valleys had been sown in dragons' teeth the night before they could not have poured in faster or seemingly more out of nowhere. For the messengers carried stirring words of high drama, such drama as one is seldom granted to witness in real life, and as the messengers went into every nook and corner the whole countryside for many miles around dropped their tools and came hurrying in as one man to see and hear this thing that was reported to be happening in their midst.

But in the center of the multitude stood three grim figures who neither moved nor stirred out of their places nor spoke to anyone. There were the makers of this weird drama who kept watch by the casket in which reposed the earthly remains of the lonely heroine whose spirit was presently to suffuse the multitude with such a feeling of awe and wonder as her living presence could never have done. But since Patton's role was purely professional, his duty as an officer of the law being to see that the law was observed and no physical violence was done, let us pass over him to glance briefly at the other two as they stood poised for the final clash in their deadly struggle.

Pale and trembling, Young stood as one transfixed, seemingly oblivious to all about him but actually supremely alive. From the beginning he had believed that his dream had been given to him for a purpose, and in that belief his faith had never once wavered. Doubtless the responsibility of the multitude weighed heavily upon him; and doubtless, too, the grandeur of the struggle and the realization that it was a struggle to the death awed and humbled him. But for him the great moral issues had already been solved—they were solved the moment that he looked into the casket and recognized the face of the corpse as the face of the young woman who had stood before him and cried for help— and his mind was free from stress and his whole being pulsed with joy in the consciousness that he was doing right. He was seeking neither to implicate Effler nor to vindicate himself but to do his duty as he understood it, and he had to do that regardless of whom it hurt and though all the world opposed him; and as he stood now and looked toward the future he had only one fear, and that was a fear that could wait—the fear that the McDowell officer would make the same mistake that the coroner had.

But whereas Young had only one fear, Effler had only one hope. We can only guess at the wild turmoil of his mind and the clash of his fears and alarms. Outwardly he had achieved a semblance of composure and tried to appear calm and indifferent—his very life, he felt, depended upon it—but inwardly he was in a turmoil of bitterness and despair and wild surmises. Perhaps for the thousandth time he assured himself that he had nothing to fear for his person, that he had left no marks on his wife's body and no court of law would convict him on the evidence of a dream. But it was no use. These men knew something. He had somehow stumbled into the clutches of a grand conspiracy, and the dream was only a ruse to draw him out and make him witness against himself. But the more he tried to fathom the mystery of it the more bewildered and terrified he became. His whole being was swallowed up by fear; and he was afraid to move or speak lest he betray himself; all he could do was stand astounded and try to force a wan smile.

To make his position more untenable, the sympathy of the multitude now swung from him to Young and he sensed it. Two factors had combined to bring this about. The first was Young's superhuman courage in standing forth alone against great odds. People admire courage wherever they find it, and Young's dramatic stand in the name of the law electrified the crowd and made him a hero on the instant. The other was Effler himself. People don't like to be caught supporting the losing party, particularly when the losing party proclaims itself to be the wrong party, and Effler's evident distress clearly revealed that he had more to fear than he had made known.

But the most dramatic change in the complex of the multitude was yet to come. From the beginning they had had the feeling that what they were witnessing was high drama, and to this feeling was now added a sense of the supernatural. How it came about no one knew, and it doesn't matter; all that matters is that the dream began to be believed, and with belief it seemed as if the spirit of the young woman returned in triumph and breathed upon them the breath of conviction in herself. The response was miraculous. The dream was no longer a dream but a living force, a manifestation of the Divine—and such a feeling of awe and wonder passed over them as they had never experienced before. They walked on tiptoe and spoke in awed, hushed voices, but it was not the awe and hush of a funeral but of rapture; at last they had become one with Young and aliens to Effler and waited in the deliriousness of high expectancy.

The afternoon lengthened into evening without other incident, and the crag-spangled sunset purpled the autumn-blushed hills and filled the deepening west with a burning zone of fire from which long spreading bars of amber streamed outward in all directions. Ordinarily when the people of the mountains take note of this familiar natural phenomenon of the departing day they say it is the sun drawing up water to make rain, but this evening no one was conscious of the flight of time or gave a thought to the grandeur of the scene. People were arriving now from as far away as Mitchell County, Marion, and the middle reaches of Yancey. Evening softened into twilight and twilight into dusk, and to the twinkling of the stars was added the eerie glimmer of many sparkling campfires which the multitude got going to break the autumn chill of night.

Finally, through the dark, came the long-awaited cry, "The doctor! The doctor! Make way for the doctor!" The multitude parted this way and that and Dr. Virgil R. Butts, then of Marion but afterwards of Bakersville, approached, accompanied by the high sheriff of McDowell County and certain of his deputies. A young man late out of medical school, Dr. Butts asked no questions and spoke not a word but made his way to the corpse as unerringly as a lover seeks out his loved one. He demanded lights and the lamps of the Patton home were brought out. He demanded a table and the Patton dining table was brought out. He ordered the corpse taken out of the casket and laid onto the table and it was done. Then he went straight to the work, while in all the vast multitude not a foot moved nor a breath heaved; when it was finished he turned his face upward and intoned into the night, "This woman has died from a broken neck and a bruise on the back of her neck as if made by the pole of an axe." For one moment longer the awful stillness held, then the mighty voice of the multitude thundered in reply, "The woman died from a broken neck and a bruise on the back of her neck as if made by the pole of an axe!"

Effler made no attempt at flight; looking this way and that, he stood wringing his hands and whimpering that he didn't know how it had happened. But he had not long to wait; Patton arrested him on the spot as a suspect in the case—and at long last the long-suffering funeral party resumed its sorrow-laden journey. But Effler went the other way: Patton delivered him to the high sheriff of McDowell County and he went to jail. His obligation to his duty discharged, Young thanks the people for their patience and kindness and went home, the multitude dispersed and went their several ways, and the dream which that morning Young had been afraid to tell above a whisper lest it be overheard and fall into the hands of the local interpreters went that night into the hearts of a wonder-stricken people from one end of the Toe River Valley to the other. But Young had himself unknowingly supplied the interpretation. He himself was the interpretation, both the dreamer and the doer chosen by Heaven that the wicked might not slay with impunity, and for many years thereafter the people kept fresh in story and turned with increased fear and devotion to Him Whose Word is wonderful, whose ways are unsearchable and past finding out, and though in the long while since then they may have grown remiss in the latter they have never wearied of the former, and from them his story has passed to regions beyond and become one of the great stories of the Southern mountains and is listened to with awe and wonder wherever good stories are told.

Effler went out of hearing proclaiming his innocence and swearing vengeance, but in the silence of his prison cell he thought better of the matter and confessed to his guilt. The dream played no part in the court action against him; he was tried, convicted and sentenced to hang on his own written confession. From first to last he denied that he used any instrument in the slaying other than the strip of cloth herein described, and the supposition is that he broke his wife's neck and made the bruise with his clenched fist as he twisted. He was hanged by public execution at high noon on May 19, 1982, at Marion, North Carolina, county seat of McDowell County. As the day approached he grew darkly remorseful and maintained to the end, even to his last words on the scaffold, that he would not die of a broken neck but by choking; as he had purposed to kill his wife so would he die, he said—and, oddly enough, by a strange coincidence in the hangman's art, he partly caught the force of his weight as he fell, and when his body was taken down it was found that he had died, not of a broken neck, but by strangulation as he swung in midair. Thus was fulfilled the last grim prediction in this weird drama in which Heaven interposed and life was paid for by life. The End.

V. DOCUMENTS

[Author's note: On Dec. 27, 2000, I had all 114 pages of the trial documents relating to State v. Stephen Effler copied at the North Carolina Supreme Court Archives in Raleigh. Most of that number are printed forms for subpoenas; some are lists of names of jurors for the venire. I have attempted to re-assemble the documents in chronological order. I have included the lists of names of the witnesses subpoenaed; however, I have not reproduced the printed forms for those subpoenas because they contain no relevant information except the witnesses' names.]

COMPLAINT

McDowell County

S.C. Turner being duly Sworn Complains on oath to W.F. Craig J.P. that he is informed that Steven Effler did on the night of the 6th day of January 1881 kill his (Steven Effler's) wife, And this Complainant further says that the said Steven Effler did on the day aforesaid maliciously commit said Criminal Offense and he prays that a proper warrant issue to the end that the said person Steven Effler be brought before a magistrate to be dealt with according to law.

Sworn and Subscribed}   S.C. Turner

To before me}
This the 10th day Jany}
1881
W.F. Craig, J.P.

WARRANT FOR EFFLER'S ARREST

McDowell County Before W.F. Craig J.P.

State}	
Against	Warrant for
Steven Effler}	Murder

The State of North Carolina—
To any lawful officer of McDowell County. Greeting.

Whereas complaint has been made before me this day on the oath of S.O. [sic] Turner that he is informed that Steven Effler did on the night of the 6th day of January 1881 wickedly and unlawfully kill his own wife, and that the said Steven Effler did with force and arms, at and in the County aforesaid unlawfully and wilfully Commit the said Criminal offense Against the peace and dignity of the State.

These are therefore to command you to forthwith apprehend the said Steven Effler and him hard before me at Marion in Marion Township McDowell County, N.C. then and there to answer the said Charge and be dealt with according to law. Given under my hand and seal the lOth day of January 1881

W.F. Craig, J.P.

[NOTES on back of above]

STATE

Against
Steven Effler
Recd lOth Jany 1881
I depute S. C.Turner Merrett Burgin [?] Patton & Stickland McFalls to serve this warrant. J.G. Neal Shff.,

Served by arrresting Steven Effler & Bringing him before W.F. Craig
JP for trial Jany 12th 1881
JG Neal Sheriff
SC Turner

The defendant be committed to jail to await his trial at the Spring
Term of McDowell Superior Court This the 12th day of Jany 1881
W.F. Craig JP

Witnesses for State
V.R. Butt M.D.
Isaac Green
John Carson
S.M. Burgin
Ed Sowers
John M. Burgin
Joshua Young
Elz. Burnett
Jane Johnson
John Simmons Jun.

WITNESSES FOR EFFLER

[I have not copied most of the printed subpoena forms; however, this is the only place where I found the names of the witnesses
for Effler: Lyaid [Lydia] McFalls, Bitty McFalls, Polly Effler,
Cathrine Lanning, George Robinson, Sandy Patton, Stephen
Ballew. Clinton Carraway was subpoenaed from Madison County.
Clinton Carraway apparently was already living with Effler's
mother because one of the witnesses referred to her as "Polly
Carraway." Polly Effler and Clinton Carraway were married in
1885.

[Yet another one shows yet another set of witnesses called before
the Grand Jury: Noah McFalls, Charles Cresawn, Gavin Lanning, Jeff
Lanning, Martha Effler, Sadie Lanning, and Rebecca Sowers. John

N.B. Smith was also called as witness, but there is no indication as to which side called him.]

THE INDICTMENT

State of North Carolina}

Superior Court McDowell County} Spring Term 1881
The jurors for the State upon their oath present that Stephen Efler late of the County of McDowell, Laborer, not having the fear of God before his eyes but being moved and seduced by the instigation of the devil on the Sixth day of January in the year of Our Lord One Thousand Eight Hundred and Eighty One with force and arms at and in the county aforesaid in and upon one Peggie Efler in the peace of God and the state then and there being feloniously willfully and of his malice aforethought did make an assault; and that the said Stephen Efler then and there feloniously wilfully and of his malice aforethought-did strike beat kick and choke the said Peggie Efler with both his hands and feet in and upon the head nose neck side and other parts of the body of her the said Peggie Efler and there and then feloniously wilfully and of his malice aforethought did

Cast and throw the said Peggie Efler down upon and unto the ground with great violence then, giving unto the said Peggie Efler then and there as well by the beating striking kicking and choking of her the said Peggie Efler in manner and form aforesaid as by the casting and throwing of her the said Peggie Efler down as aforesaid several mortal bruses and fractures in and upon the head, nose, neck and side of her the said Peggie Efler of which said Mortal bruises and fractures of which the said Peggie Effler then and their instantly died. And so the jurors aforesaid upon their oath aforesaid do say that the said Stephen Efler the said Peggie Efler in manner and form aforesaid feloniously wilfully and ofhis malice aforethought did kill and murder contrary to the form of the statutes in such case made and provided and against the peace and dignity of the state.

And the jurors aforesaid upon their oath aforesaid do further present that the said Stephen Efler not having the fear of God before his eyes but being moved and deduced by the instigation of the devil Afterwards to wit on the said Sixth day of January in the year of Our Lord one thousand.Eight Hundred and Eighty one with force and arms at and in the county of McDowell aforesaid in and upon one Peggie Efler in the peace of God and the state then and there being feloniously wilfully and of his malice aforethought did make an assault; and in some way and manner and by some means to the person aforesaid unknown feloniously wilfully and of his malice aforethought did strike and beat her the said Peggie Efler in and upon the head neck nose and left side of her the said Peggie Efler giving to her the said Peggy Efler three mortal wounds bruises and fractures in and upon the nose neck and left side and breaking the neck,

of her the said Peggie Efler each of the depth of three inches and of the breadth of one inch of which said mortal bruises and fractures and breaking of the neck the said Peggie Efler there and then instantly died. And so the jurors aforesaid upon their oath aforesaid do say that that [sic] the said Stephen Efler the said Peggie Efler in manner and form aforesaid feloniously and wilfully and of his malice aforethought did kill and murder contrary to the form of the statute in such case made and proved and against the peace and dignity of the state
J.S. Adams, Sol.

[NOTES on outside of document]

State vs.
Stephen Effler,

Indictment Murder
Gov Pros
Witnesses
Ed Sowers &
Joshua Young
S M Burgin
Isaac Greer

John M. Burgin
Ells Burnett
Ruth Burnett
& Jane Johnson
John Simmons
Dr. Whittington &
Dr. V.R. Butt

Subpoenaed from Yancey: D.N. Shuford, John McNeal, James Bird (colored), Bettie McFalls, Mary Cresawn and Martha Grindstaff

From Mitchell: Lucy Grindstaff. Also from Madison: Henry Efler Jr. From Rutherford: Dr. E.B. Harris

---

Effler's petition for a postponement to the Fall Term of Superior Court

North Carolina} Superior Court
McDowell} Spring Term 1881

State}
Vs.   Murder
Stephen Effler}

The Defendant after being duly sworn says that he cannot come safely to the trial of his cause during the present term as he is advised and believes First—his Co unsel advise him that they have been unable and will be unable to prepare his defense at this time on account of matters of law which they have not had the time or opportunity to examine & second that he is advised & believes partys have influenced and many men of standing & influence in this County have denounced affiant's cause and prejudiced the public mind to that extent that he fears he cannot have a fair trial at this time—Third—That Defendant has used all the diligence he could to be ready, but now finds as he is advised by his counsel witnesses that are material & necessary for his defense have not been subpoenaed because their materiality was not known to affiant or his counsel & could not be known except upon the examination of the States evidence—That this affidavit is not made for delay but for the causes therein stated and to obtain a fair trial.

Sworn to & subscribed}   Stephen X [his mark] Effler
Before me March 30,1881}
DOHW Gillespie Clerk Supr Court

JURORS

State of North Carolina} Superior Court
McDowell County} Fall Term 1881

State
Against}   Murder
Stephen Efler}

To the Sheriff of McDowell County Greeting

In obedience to an order of the Court in this case, you are hereby commanded to summon a special venire of Sixty good and lawful men to be and appear here that is to say at this place Thursday September the 29th 1881 at 9 o'clock 30 minutes A.M. to serve as a special Venire of Jurors in this case.

Given under my hand and seal of office, this 27th day of September 1881
D.O.H. W. Gillespie CSC

First Venire of 60 men:

1. Amos Hensly; 2. J.W. Hemphill; 3. John Q. Morrison; 4. S. W. Blalock; 5. L. B. Hemphill; 6. J.L. Silver; 7. John Hensly; 8. Wm. Dellinger; 9. J.C. Sandlin; 10. Thos Dobson; 11. L.C. Blackwelder; 12. F.M. Hensly; 13. Dan'l Queen; 14. John Seagle; 15. J.F. Patton; 16. J.W. Grant; 17. John Holland; 18. Wm A. McCall; 19. J.W. Hunter; 20. W.M. Dobson; 21. Thos Y. Lytle; 22. Jno H. Finly; 23. Henry Shirlin; 24. H.S. Poteet; 25. J.H.C. Gillespie; 26. Wm Wilkerson; 27. Jno A. Shuford; 28. R. L. Vaughn; 29. Geo Sattlemire; 30. A.H. Simmons; 31. H.H. Taylor; 32. Wm Hensly; 33. J.P. Norton; 34. Z. S. Hawkins; 35. N.C. Finly; 36. Wm Walton; 37. J.M. McCoy; 38. James R. McCelvy; 39. Wm C. Elliott; 40. Jno Hainey; 41. A.C. Gardin; 42. Isaac Stacy; 43. G.W. Lacky; 44. D.M. Washburn; 45. Wilford Huskins; 46. A.S. Barnes; 47. J.K. Hawkins; 48. Jno W. Price; 49. Noah Yount; 50. J. Mills Lytle; 51. W.A. Conley; 52. Jacob Knipe; 53. Frank Morrison; 54. Wm. McNeely; 55. Dan'l Holland Sr.; 56. J.M. Reel; 57. Thos A. White; 58. P.F. Simmons; 59. C.F. Pyatt; 60. J.L. Burgin.

State of North Carolina
McDowell County

State}
Against}   Murder   Supr Court
Stephen Effler}   Fall Term 1881

To the Sheriff of McDowell County Greeting

In obedience to an order of the Court in this case, You are hereby commanded to summon a Special Venire of Fifty good and lawful men to be and appear here that is to say at this place Thursday, September the 29th 1881 at 2 O'Clock 30 minutes P.M. to serve as a special venire of Jurors in this case.

Given under my hand and seal of office, this 29th day of Sept 1881. D.O.H.W. Gillespie CSC

Second venire of 50 men:

1. Thos Hemphill; 2. Thos Y. Greenlee; 3. Amos Horton; 4. Henry Hawk; 5. Sam'l Deal; 6. I. J. Morton; 7. R.P. Holyfield; 8. W.D. Gray; 9. J.C. Evans; 10. W.F. Craig; 11. W.B. Grant; 12. Levy Austin; 13. E.W. Morton; 14. C.P. Raidar; 15. J.P. Cansler; 16. Phillip Burnett; 17. R.H. Laster; 18. J.W. Marsh; 19. Wm Fleming; 20. Jno D. Hall; 21. J.C. Curtis; 22. Benj. Seagle; 23. Wm Powell; 24. Harvy Price; 25. I.J. Hallar; 26. John Lytle; 27. F.M. Harris; 28. Benj. Bird; 29. W.M. Ledbetter; 30. Geo McCormac; 31. G.M. Lytle; 32. M.L. Kayler; 33. G.W. Conly; 34. J.P. Finly; 35. James Ballew; 36. David Walker; 37. David Hall; 38. Wm M. Blanton; 39. John Pyatt; 40. W.W. Baily; 41. J.D. Gibson; 42. Jno McCurry; 43. W.H. Moody; 44. James Lacky; 45. G.H. Gardin; 46. J.C. Pool; 47. W.L. Morrison; 48. J. H. Duncan; 49. James S. Elliott; 50. James M. Hall.

JURORS CHOSEN TO HEAR THE CASE

George Cayler, John Holland, R.T. Vaughn, J.K. Hawkins, G.W. Lackey, J.P. Norton, C.F. Pyatt, William Dobson, Thomas Dobson, George W. Conley, J.W. Marsh, John Lytle.

NOTES ON THE TESTIMONY OF WITNESSES AT THE TRIAL

[Note: the following notes on witness' testimony are very rough. There was a loose page among the documents that said, "Judge's Notes" and that could be what this first set of notes is.]

 State}
 Vs}   Murder
 Stephen Efler}

Gavan Lanning says I was at Henry Eflers, Prs. [abbreviation of prisoner's?] Grandfather, and Prs. Came there in the night. The dogs were barking and he hallowed before he got to the house I was in bed and didn't hear what he said. We told him to come to house & he came and said Peggy is about dead and I want you all to go over there. He called John Efflers wife and said Peggy said for her to go and shake hands with her. He said in reply to H. Effler's question. She is as dead as she can be. When asked how she was effected he stated she complained of her head and neck that she had a spell that [like] the one she had along in the summer. For awhile after Steve was married he seemed not to talk to her & this caused some talk in the country & I asked him if he was jealous of her and he said no he would tell me some time what the matter was. I assisted in dressing her. I did not discover any bones were broken. While we were there old man E said in Steve's presence I will go and get John Burgin and Dave Byrd to examine her there may be some talk that Steve killed her. When I first saw her she had on no clothes except an outside shirt and a sack her breast was exposed

JEFF LANNING

I was at old man Es when Steve came he hallowed and said (I think) Peggie is dead after stating about as foregoing witness he states that Steve said on the road that she was complaining of her neck and head. On one occasion I heard Steve curse his wife threaten [?] to knock her down if she did not hush and say if there was no one with me you would be afraid to talk.

CHARLES CRESAWN

I went to Steves house on Sat night after death saw dead body held the light and noticed that neck was very limber. When I got there blood was running out of her nose and mouth. Saw a bruise under right eye. Her neck was bruised

NOAH MCFALLS

Discharged

ELDRIDGE BURNETT

Speaks of appearance of body.

JOHN SIMMONS

I was on the Yancey Coroners Jury

WM BYRD

Saw corpse bleeding at nose and mouth neck limber.

EDWARD SO WERS

Came to steve Effler's house on the night of 6th of Jan. Went in the House. Steve's wife was at the table sowers asked how she was, she says "I am as well as common." Steve told his wife to fix supper for sowers, she did so. Sowers took supper with Effler Steve's said she was going to her father's Steve said she should not go. Sowers stayed awhile, and went home. Steve Effler came to sower's house in about three hours and told him his wife was very sick. Sowers got up and went with Effler to his house when they entered the Effler called his wife and she did not answer. Effler said she was dead. Sowers went to the bed with a light saw she was dead he asked steve to hold the light Steve did so. She was lying straight in the bed, on her back, but her neck was twisted. Sowers run his hand under her face to straighten it and got blood on his hand, he thinks her neck was broken.

RUTHY BURNETT

Saw condition of body on Saturday after death Every time anyone would go near the botty Effler would watch their motion but not act so when any of his family would go.

REBECCA SOWERS

It was two or three hours from the time Mr. Sowers came home from Efflers until she got there nose was running bloody froth. Saw two damp chemises hanigng on a pole in the house Effler told Mr. Sowers his wife could not get up and was past speaking

LUCINDA SMITH

LUCINDA SMITH [the name is thus repeated but no testimony is recorded]

JNO. L.B. SMITH

Effler told Smith that he allowed to go to Tennessee that he did not intend to work a family, and that Peggy could go where she please That Effler was teasing his wife about going to see other girls. And they had some words. Smith could not hear the words Effler jerked her pocket off.

JANE JOHNSON

Steve Effler mother told told [sic] Jane Johnson that she believed that she Peggy Effler's head was tore all to peace inside for when "I move it something makes a noise like water sushing.

J.M. BURGIN

Steven E told Mr. Burgin that she taken with a pain in her head something like a fit and that she fought as long as she was able and he lead [laid] on the bed the bed [sic] and went to his grand fathers and she was laying when he returned just as he had left her

S.W. BURGIN

Peggy Effler was very black in the face and her neck was limber

MARGARETTE LANDEN

She saw the body the night she died. Close [clothes] some of them were wet.

MARTHA EFFLER

Saw the body the night she died

MORE COMPLETE NOTES ON TESTIMONY AT THE TRIAL

State Vs Stephen Efler

ED SOWERS BY STATE:

On 6th Jany last I lived in Yancy foot of Blue Ridge in Yancey County—Stephen Efler lived 1 ½ miles from me at foot of Blue Ridge on McDowell side—Henry Efler grand father of Stephen lived 1 mile beyond me. Peggy Efler lived with Stephen & was considered his wife.

I went to Marion on 6th—On my way home I passed Steph's house a little afer dark. I called & he answered. He asked me to come in & rest. He was at hog pen. When I went in his wife was at table with a child in her lap she said she was as well as usual

I eat supper. She waited on me. We sat by the fire after supper talking. She said she believed she would go to her father's next day. Steph said she couldn't go that he had to work on the mill next day. She said she had not been there in a long time—nothing unusual—I went home sat up right smart while then went to bed might have been an hour might have been…heard a noise as of something running through—no fence—After a while I heard some one at door some one spoke—I didn't answer. Called again—said get up & go with us to Stephen Efler's his wife was powerful sick—They all came in—Jeff. Burwin, Margret Lanning, Martha Efler, & Peggy Grindstaff & deft—

Stephen Efler said to me to go with him. He was uneasy. That Jeff could come with women.
He said she appeared out of her head
That she was having something like fits

When we got near the house, he said what is that I said I thought it was hogs. He walked with his hand on my shoulder from fence to house when he got to house he said Oh Peggy No answer. He walked towards bed don't know whether he touched Peggy or not—turned back to me & said she was dead I said no surely. He said yes—what will I do
He bald down & cried or let on he was crying. I light fire. Went to woman put my hand on her. Felt she was getting cold. He asked me to see if child was dead. I touched it & it woke up. He took it up.

She was laying on her back a little turned to right her face towards child-her left arm was over her breast—right arm towards child—her clothing came above her waist that she had only a black sack open—no shirt on I straightened her head & closed her eyes & mouth touched her no more till the women came—I saw bloody froth running out of her nose & in her mouth—Her neck was limber could turn it very easy—color of her face was red or purple. I didn't see any bruises.

Stephens mother Polly Carraway dresssed her Catherine Lanning her sister helped. I stayed till about day—came back next Friday night & stayed till about morning. She was put in a coffm Saturday night. We carried her over the Mountain on…to Stephen Efler carried it carefully—Head foremost up the mountain feet foremost down.

He said she said she would lie with him, if he wouldn't let her go to her fathers. There was an axe under bed. She didn't have the dress on she had when I was there before   no   [number] years before. [He said—words marked out] I worked with. He said he wasn't going to live with her. She was good to him as she could be to a baby. He said the reason he wasn't going to live with her was he didn't love her.

X [Cross-examination by defense] Saw him frequently after he said he didn't love his wife. He was very kind to her. There was some wet clothing hanging up. I remember seeing 2 wet shirts hung up.

CHARLES CRESAWN BY STATE

I remember when Polly [sic] Efler died it was on a Thursday. I went then on Saturday. Her father Joseph Grindstaff asked me to go & help bring her across the mountains. She lay on the bed. I helped put her in coffm. She looked very dark. Her neck was very limber. Blood ran out of her nose. Noticed nothing wrong about her head. It sort of…that a cloth was tied around her neck. I saw it. Her neck was a dark purple color. I saw no bruises unless there was one under her eye. That looked more red than rest of her face was dark—didn't say it was purple. Stephen left her & stayed a while or came back (after they were married) while he was gone she stayed at Henry Eflers. I aint certain think he left her twice if so she stayed with her father. I saw him while he was living with her. I asked him what was the differences between him & his wife. He said he had nothing against her didn't know as he would ever live with her again—Don't know as he was living with her then

X This was a year before she died I saw her by fire light.

JEFF LANNING BY STATE

I was at grandfather Eflers the night of Peggy's death. Steph Efler came there about 9 p.m. or later & hollered. I understood him to say Peggy was dead though the dogs were barking so I wasn't sure what he said. He hollered again & said Peggy was dying. We went, some of the girls—stopped & got…I asked him in the road what she was complaining of She said of her neck & head hurting. I don't know that I ever saw him abuse her. I heard a little quarreling one night. I have heard him say he was going to leave her—that he didn't like her or wasn't going to live with her. I heard him say he thought he'd love her after he married her—did at time He went about with her to neighbors & sometimes to church

JOSEPH GRINDSTAFF BY STATE:

Father of Peggy Efler Stephens wife.

I was there a time when they wouldn't sleep together. He wouldn't carry the child. He take off with other young boys. He went off a while about 3 weeks or so. I think she stayed at Henry Eflers part of the time & maybe part of time at my house. After she was dead I asked him what made him kill her. He said he didn't. I talked on & said he killed her. He didn't say he did or didn't any more. &c I asked him if she was mean to him and he said she wasn't.

Recalled while Dr. being examined I wasn't present at conversation between dr. & Stephen What I said was some days [sic]

ELDRIDGE BURNETT BY STATE:

Live in Yancey County 3 miles from Stephen Eflers. Went to Stephens on Saturday after she died. She looked very dark, her face & hands. Didn't see her neck. Saw some blood in her nostrils & on a cloth that lay on her breast. She didn't look natural. She looked swelled about her face & mighty dark. Saw Stephen. He appeared to want to hear what was said. He was listening & watching the people out of doors. He didn't appear to pay any attention to her as a man should to his wife at church & Sunday school. Did go or come with her once that I saw.

RUTH BURNETT BY STATE:

Was at Stephen Eflers on Saturday with my husband. Her face & hands looked very dark. Her left jaw and left ear darker than rest ofher face. Her mother had charge. I felt about her head & neck only found that she was swelled powerfull. Her head & shoulders closer together than was usual. Her chin stuck towardsher breast. Steph appeared uneasy. Would get up when we went to look at corpse.

JANE JOHNSON BY STATE:

I went there at request. In hurry. Found her laid...Polly said I believe that womans head is busted all to pieces inside for when I move it I hear it scoush in there just like water. She was very dark. I said Polly theres blood on her nose. When she said as why He was present & could hear. Steph had nothing to say-sat on a bench with his head down. Was crying some. Next day he & Polly talked for a quarter of an hour. Peggy & Steph didn't get along very 'good. Don't think he treated her as a man ought to his wife. He didn't go to preaching together. One time they didn't sleep together.

X Her hands were purple on Friday black Saturday Her head black under the eyes on Saturday.

MARTHA GRINDSTAFF BY STATE:

I was a sister of Peggy—I stayed with them a month. He didn't get her anything to eat. He talked ill to her. I don't know what the difficulty was. He left her when baby was born. I was there. He came back shortly after. Grandma & his mothers brothers wife were there.

LUCY GRINDSTAFF BY STATE:

Was at Henry Eflers Steph hollered & said Peggy was dying or dead. I went over when we got there she was dead. He said at Henry's that she complained of her head & that she couldn't get her breath.

J.M. BURGIN BY STATE

On Friday Henry Efler came to my house & asked me to go to his grandson & examine Stephen Efler's wife. I first talked to Stephen-asked him what ailed her. He said she took a spasm or fit & he held on to her until she was disabled & then he went to her grandfathers. He said she fought him & pulled his hair as long as she was able to do anything & then he laid her on the bed & started for her grandfather.

The skin of her head was very [?]. & it felt swelled—under her eyes thick—thick settled around. Didn't look at her neck. Never lifted her head.

X He said she was complaining of her head.

JOSHUA YOUNG BY STATE:

I noticed the blood from her nose. Noticed a bruise under her left eye & towards her ear. When I raised her her head went back and it seemed to me as if her head went back & struck her back. I told a young man named Jameson & told him to raise her head level with her body. Which he did. When we put her in the coffin her left side fell lower than her body. I was confident her neck was broken. Deft. was making a fuss. Didn't see any…[?]…He looked scared. Saw him look towards [?]

MARY CRESAWN BY STATE:

Saw deceased on Saturday I felt her over her ribs…her left side gave in on other side not. I pulled her ear. It peared like her head was loose from her neck. Her stomach was swelled. Left breast sunk in. Steph' s manner was strange as if he was pestered about something.

A pig came out from under the house with their noses looked bloody. One or two.

X her head moved her neck didn't It was red blood Friday

DR. H.C. [it should be V.R.] BUTTS BY STATE

Made examination wife during—

I found the neck broken. The nose…was broken…lower jaw dislocated partial dislocation of head of humus, bone of uper arm 5th, 6th 7th ribs on right side fractured. Incised.…Length 3 inches depth 1 inch & width ½ inch on left shoulder. Various Wounds or bruises over her abdomen. Nothing matter with her breast but discoloration of skin. It would take a pretty good [traumatic blow?] to break the neck there. In my opinion these wounds were caused by external violence. How many of these wounds would have caused death in less than a day. Only the breaking of the neck. These wounds were not likely to have been produced by carrying her over the mountain. I talked with Stephen Efler.

At time of my conversation the deft. Was under arrest [sentence marked out: "there had been threats of mobbing"] His appearance was that of one in trouble. There were quite a number present. I sought the conversation. I didn't tell him it would be better for him to make a statement. It was after the inquest had been held in next room. There were not over a dozen in room, most women, his mother among them.

SANDY PATTON BY DEFT:

There was a considerable excitement in crowd. I don't know that anything was said in Stephens presence about mobbing him. I didn't hear any thing said in his hearing about mobbing him

—Court holds as a fact no evidence of duress fear threats promises—Exception

DR. BUTTS

I asked him if she ever had fits, he said no. I asked him if her health was generally pretty good, said yes, excepting she occasionally couldn't eat breakfast. That night he said they had gone to bed. She woke him up by taking on. He saw that she was in bad condition & that he got up—went to his grandfathers

X The blow was from right—dislocated to left. Head would naturally pull either way.

The wound on shoulder could have been produced by something similar to an axe. If it had been an axe it would have fractured the bones this was not done. It couldn't have been produced by a knife. In the wound in ribs the blood was of an external not venous character. If wound is inflicted during life blood will be of arterial character. If after death venous character

A kick would produce injuries like those on ribs. It might have been possible if she had been in convulsion that she might have fallen back over the head board of bed & broken her neck. Death is supposed to be immediate when breaking the neck. There would have been some movement. There might have been some kicking. I never saw any thing of the kind.

X These wounds were in my opinion as an expert inflicted before death.

STATE RESTS

STEPHEN EFLER BY DEFT—

We had been asleep about an hour—She woke me up pulling my hair & poking about. I pulled her down asked her what was the matter She gave me no answer—I then went to grandfathers—When I came back she was dead—was gone about an hour. She was alive when I left. I don't remember in what position she was but she lay in bed when I left.

X I went to bed 15 minutes after Sowers left. I had been asleep about a quarter of an hour when she woke me up—She fell back towards head of bed don't know whether she struck any thing—didn't hear her head pop—Didn't hear her strike any thing.

ED SOWERS BY DEFT.

The house was a log cabin—inside hewed. Bed in one corner, head against side of house—didn't notice how close to wall—baby next to wall at side of bed.

ELD. BURNETT BY DEF.

Small log house, setting west &c.

MARGARET LANNING BY DEF.

It was a common bedstead—not fastened to wall—house hewn inside. As far as I recollect logs were close together

ED SOWERS

Two years before her death Steve said he wasn't going to live with her—said she was as good to him as to a baby. That the reason he wasn't going to live with her was because he didn't love her.

X Saw him often after that. He was very kind to her. Steven left her once or twice for a short time.

CHAS CRESAWN

—A year before she died, I asked him what the difference between him & his wife was. He said he had nothing against her—didn't know if he would ever live with her again.

JEFF LANNING

—Don't know that I ever saw him abuse her heard a little quarrelling one night. Have heard him say he was going to leave her didn't like her & wasn't going to live with her. He went about with her some to church…

JOSEPH GRINDSTAFF Father in law

He wouldn't carry the child—had been there when they wouldn't sleep together—when they went to church, he would take off by himself—went off once for 3 weeks

ELDRIDGE BURNETT

—Didn't appear to pay any attention to her as a man should do—at church & Sunday school—never saw him with her but once

JANE JOHNSON

—Polly [sic] & Steve didn't get along very good. Didn't treat her as he ought—didn't go to preaching with her—one time didn't sleep together.

MARTHA GRINDSTAFF

He didn't get her any thing to eat. Talked ill to her He wasn't present when the baby was born—did get her bread & milk—

APPEAL TO THE SUPREME COURT OF NORTH CAROLINA

[Note: The judge himself actually wrote the appeal to the Supreme Court, based on the "exceptions" the defense lawyer had made to the judge's rulings in the case.]

State}   McDowell County

Vs}   Fall Term 1881
Stephen Efler}   Case for Supreme Court

This was an indictment for murder tried before Seymour J. and a jury at Fall Term 1881 of McDowell Superior Court.

A juror [blank space] Hunter being examined by the defendant on a challenge for cause was asked by defendants counsel whether he had formed and expressed an opinion as to the guilt or innocence of the prisoner and replied that he had—Whereupon prisoners counsel assigned this answer as a ground of challenge either principal or to the [unclear word]

The court held that the prisoner had not been shown to have formed or expressed an opinion that was unfavorable to the prisoner and that therefore the prisoner had shown no cause of challenge The court at the same time suggested to the prisoners counsel that he might ask the normal questions viz Have you formed expressed an opinion that the prisoner is guilty in any Similar question The defendants counsel declined to ask witness any further questions. Excepted and then challenged the juror peremptorily. When the prisoner accepted the 12th juror he had not exhausted his peremptory challenges having only challenged peremptorily eleven jurors.

II. The prisoner went upon the stand as a witness in his own behalf. The state offered for the purpose of discrediting him as a witness and for no other purpose to introduce evidence of defendants character. Def. Objected and the evidence was admitted by the court for the purpose specified. Defendant duly excepted.

III. A witness Dr. Butts was examined upon a conversation between himself and defendant. He defts counsel objected and proposed to show duress-and were allowed to examine Dr. Butts and one Sandy Patton on the subject. Dr. Buts testified that at the time of the conversation deft was under arrest: his appearance was that of one in trouble-there were quite a number, but not over twelve, in the room of whom his mother was one—It was just after an inquest had been had been [sic] held in the next room. I sought the conversation. I did not tell him that it would be better for him to make a Statement—

Sandy Patton testified in answer to defts questions that there was a considerable excitement in the crowd and that something had been said about mobbing the prisoner: but that he had not heard anything of the kind said in prisoners hearing or know of anything of the kind said in his presence.

X The court held that there was no evidence of threats promises or duress—The def excepted to the admission of the testimony which was as follows I asked him if she (his wife) ever had fits-he said no—I asked him if her health was generally good he said yes Excepting that she could not occasionally eat breakfast. That night he said they had gone to bed: that she woke him up by taking on—he saw that she was in bad condition and went for help to his grandfather's

For the purpose of Explaining this and the following exception the following statement of facts is given.

The deceased and defendant were husband and wife and lived alone-a baby of 8 months with them—in a log house on the South side of the foot of the Blue Ridge. A neighbor eat supper with them on the night of the alleged homicide and a little while after dark left them and went home—about an...a mile & a half off on the other side of the mountain-an hour or so afterwards he was awakened by def who said his wife was very badly off. He and a number of others went with deft home—and found deceased dead—Dr. Butts testified that her neck was broken, three of her ribs were broken, her shoulder out of joint bruises on her abdomen and an incised...3 inches long one inch deep on her right shoulder. She was found lying on the bed, her head turned partly towards her baby—a sack on but no "shirt"— her wet "shirts" were hung up in the room to dry—no blood found on her person save some in her nostrils or mouth. The theory of the defense was that she had a fit and fell over the bed-& broke her neck. Deft had told [words crossed out: several witnesses that] a witness J.M. Burgin so he testified that deceased had a spasm or fit & he held her until she was disabled & then he went to his grandfathers & Ed Sowers testified that deft said she had something like fits

Jeff Lanning said deft told him deceased was complaining that her neck and head hurt—

X Lucy Grindstaff said def told her that deceased complained of her head & that she couldn't get her breath. The above statements except that of Burgin witnesses testified were made to them by deft when he came over the Ridge and asked for assistance—stating that his wife was badly off

4. The following testimony was introduced by the state and given without objection. A witness Mary Cresawn testified that she heard a noise under the house of dogs or pigs...a couple of pigs came out from under the house where deceased died with blood on their

noses—it looked like fresh blood—was red—This was on Saturday the time of the alleged homicide was on Thursday night—this was the last testimony given. Deft moved on the day after the testimony was admitted at the opening of court to strike it out as irrelevant. Motion refused

State contended that def had washed the shirt of dec'd in water & put it under the house & that pigs had put their noses in this water [line marked out: "was said about this testimony by the state in its argument or by the judge in his charge."]

There was besides the evidence set forth above Evidence given as to the manner in which deft and deceased lived together—on the question of motive Evidence as to the appearance of deceased and as to manner of the prisoner after the alleged crime.

No exceptions were taken to the charge.

Verdict guilty of murder.

Move for new trial denied. Sentence of death.

Appeal prayed granted.

Deft in aff. Allowed to appeal without giving security.

Case for Supreme Court

Aug. J. Seymour, S.C.

NOTICE OF APPEAL

North Carolina}
McDowell County} Superior Court
Fall term 1881

State}
v.   Murder
Stephen Effler}

The defendant Stephen Effler maketh oath, that a verdict has been rendered against me in the above entitled cause or criminal action at the term of the court aforesaid & judgment thereon has followed in due course of law, that being dissatisfied therewith, I have after excepting, appealed to the Supreme Court of North Carolina at its next term—I also swear that I am advised by counsel that I have good cause of appeal. I further swear that I am poor & am unable to give the bond required by law, or to make any deposit whatsoever to…the costs of appeal and I further swear that I have made due diligence to comply with the law in such cases

Sworn to & subscribed by Stephen effler

Before me Octo 5 1881

D.O.H. W. Gillespie CSC

SUPREME COURT AFFIRMS THE LOWER COURT DECISION

ST ATE v. STEPHEN EFLER.

Juror-Challenge-Defendant Witness for Himself-Declarations—Trial.

1. On a trial for murder, a juror stated, in reply to the question whether he had formed and expressed an opinion as to the *guilt* or *innocence* of. the prisoner, that he had, and the prisoner challenged him for cause; thereupon the court suggested to prisoner's counsel to ask the juror whether the opinion expressed was that the prisoner was guilty, which counsel declined to do, and the challenge was disallowed: H*eld,* no error. In such case an opinion expressed constitutes good cause of challenge for that party only against whom the bias exists, and it Is encumbent on him who challenges to show himself to be the party likely to be prejudiced.

2. Where the defendant in a criminal action avails himself of the act of 1881, ch. 110, and becomes a witness in his own behalf, be thereby subjects himself to all the disadvantages of that position, in the same manner as any other witness, and may be discredited by proof of his general bad moral character.

3. Whether the declarations of a prisoner are voluntary or induced. by hope or fear, Is a question of fact to be decided by the court below, whose finding is conclusive. And the mere fact of the prisoner's making them while under arrest is not in law sufficient to exclude his declarations otherwise freely made.

4. Evidence was received without objection, and on the next day of the trial a motion to strike it out upon the ground of irrelevancy was refused: *Held,* no error. It is matter within the discretionary power of the Judge, and its exercise is not reviewable.

(*S. v. Benton,* 19 N. C., 196; S. v. *Arthur,* 13-N. C., 217; S. v. *Boswell, ib.,* 209; S. v. *O'Neale,* 26 N. C., 88; *S.v. Dove,* 32 N. C., 469; S. v. *Parks,* 25 N. C., 296; Bullinger v. *Marshall* 70 N. C., 520; *S. v. Vann* 82 N. C., 631; *S. v. Davis,* 63 N. C., 578; S. v. Houston, 76 N.C. 256; S. v. Cruse, 74 N. C., 491, cited and approved).

MURDER, tried at Fall Term, 1881, of McDowell, *Seymour,* J.

IN THE SUPREME COURT

STATE *v.* EFLER.

The prisoner was charged with the killing of Peggie Efler, his wife, on 6 January, 1881. The jury having found him guilty, he appealed from the judgment pronounced upon the verdict.

A ttorney-General for the State.

J. M. Gudger for prisoner.

RUFFIN. J. Impressed as we were with the earnestness of counsel who argued this cause before us, and realizing the immense importance to the prisoner of the issues involved, we have bestowed upon them our most earnest consideration. Having done so, and detecting nothing in the matters assigned as errors which in our opinion entitles the prisoner to another trial, it is our duty so to declare.

The first error assigned is based upon: the action of the court with reference to the juror Hunter. As appears from the record, the facts connected with that matter are as follows: When the juror was called he was challenged *for cause*—by the prisoner's counsel, and in response to a question whether he had formed and expressed an opinion as to the *guilt or innocence* of the prisoner said that he had. The counsel insisted that this constituted good cause of challenge, either principal or to the favor. His Honor held to the contrary, inasmuch as it did not appear that the opinion of the juror was unfavorable to the prisoner, but suggested to counsel to ask the juror directly whether he had formed and—expressed the opinion that the prisoner was guilty. This the counsel declined to do and, excepting to the disallowance of his challenge for cause, peremptorily challenged the Juror.

When a full jury was procured there had been only eleven peremptory challenges made on the part of the prisoner.

An opinion fully made up and expressed touching that which is the subject-matter of an action, whether civil or criminal, constitutes a good cause of principal challenge for that party only against whom the bias supposed to be created by such a declaration operates, and it is therefore encumbent on him who challenges to show himself to be the party likely to be prejudiced. *S. v. Benton,* 19 N.C., 196. The prisoner had the opportunity by putting to the juror the question suggested by the court to ascertain certainly whether the preconceived opinion of the juror was against himself, and failing to do so his mere apprehension that such might be the case gave him no good cause of challenge. Apart from this, the prisoner sustained no injury by the action of the court, admitting it to have been an error to disallow his challenge. He had the full benefit of a trial by a jury free from all exception; and this is all that the law intends to secure for him. The juror objected to was not forced upon him, and the peremptory challenge used to get rid of him was not needed for any other purpose. *S. v. Arthur* 13 N. C, 217.

Second exception: The prisoner was examined as a witness in his own behalf, and the State, for the purpose of discrediting him as a witness, and for no other purpose, offered evidence of his general bad character, and it was admitted by the court, though objected to.

The statute of 1881, ch. 110, sec. 2, provides that in the trial of all indictments against persons charged with the commission of crimes in the several courts of the State, the person charged shall at his own request, but not otherwise, *be a competent witness,* and the question is as to the effect upon the rights of a defendant who sees proper to avail himself of the privilege. In declaring him to be "a competent. witness" we understand the statute to mean that he shall occupy the same position with any other witness, be under the same obligation to tell the truth, entitled to the same privileges, receive the same protection, and equally liable to be impeached or discredited. Unless willing to become a witness, he is invested with a presumption of innocence such as the law makes in favor of every person accused of crime, and evidence cannot be offered to impeach his character unless he voluntarily puts it in issue. But by availing himself of the statute he assumes the position of a witness and subjects himself to all the disadvantages of that position, and his credibility is to be weighed and tested as that of any other witness.

This much seemed to be conceded by the counsel for the prisoner, but he insisted that the impeaching testimony should have been confined to an inquiry into the prisoner's general character for truth, and not permitted to extend to his *general moral character,* and for this position he cited us to the case of *S. V., Fletcher,* 49 Ind., 124. That case does draw the distinction suggested by counsel, but it proceeds not at all upon any idea that a difference is to be made between a defendant who testifies for himself and any other witness who might be examined in the cause; on the contrary, it distinctly recognizes the right of the prosecution to impeach the testimony of the defendant *as a. witness* by proof of his general character to be the same as in the case of any other witness, and the inquiry was limited to the reputation of the defendant for veracity merely because such was understood to be law in that State with reference to every witness.

In this State a different rule prevails, and has done so for a long series of years. In the case of *S. v. Boswell,* 13 N. C., 209, it is said that ever since the year 1804 it has been an established rule of practice in this State to discredit a witness by making proof of his gene:ral bad moral character, and that the question need not be restricted to his reputation merely for veracity. That such continues to be the law of evidence as administered in the courts of this State is shown by the following cases: *S. v. O'Neale,* 26 N. C., 88; *S. v. Dove,* 32 N. C., 469; *S.*

v. Parks, 25 N. C., 296; and, as the prisoner assumed the character of a. witness, he must needs come under the same law.

As was said *(Bullinger v. Marshall,* 70 N. C., 520) by the late Chief Justice with reference to the statute by which parties to civil actions were made competent witnesses, we have to yield to the change made in the law of evidence, and, without expressing any opinion as to its wisdom, to carry it out with all its corollaries.

The next exception was to the admission in evidence of certain declarations made by the prisoner on the evening of the coroner's inquest, he being then under arrest: When a tender of this evidence was made, the prisoner objected to its reception upon the ground that the declarations were made under circumstances of duress, and he was allowed to examine witnesses as to those circumstances. One witness testified that the declarations were made in a room next to that in which the inquest had been held, and in which there were at the time about a dozen persons, including the prisoner's mother; that no inducements either of fear or hope were held out to the prisoner,but that he, the witness, sought the conversation with him. Another witness testified that there. was a considerable crowd assembled about the place where the inquest had been held, and much excitement amongst them; and that something had been said in the crowd, though not in the presence or hearing of the prisoner about mobbing him.

Upon this evidence the court found as a fact that the declarations had been voluntarily made, free from the influence of any threats, promises or duress, and admitted the evidence.

Whether the declarations of the prisoner were voluntary or induced by hope or fear was a question of fact to be decided by his Honor, and his finding in regard thereto is conclusive. *S. v. Vann,* 82 N. C., 631; *S. v. Davis,* 63 N.C., 578. And that the mere fact of his being under arrest, at the time of making them is not of itself and as a legal conclusion sufficient to exclude, his declarations, otherwise freely made, is the well-established law of this State.

S.v *Jefferson*, 28 N. C., 305; *S. v. Houston*, 76 N.C., 256; *S. v.Cruise;* 74 N.C., 491.

The last. exception taken for the prisoner is thus stated in the case sent up: The alleged homicide occurred on. Thursday night. When found the deceased was lying on a bed with her neck broken, her shoulder dislocated, bruises on her abdomen and an incised wound three inches long and one inch deep—on the right shoulder; she had on no, underclothing, but two. wet garments were hung up in the room to dry. There was no blood "found upon her person, save Some in her mouth arid nostrils. The theory of the State was that after slaying his wife the prisoner washed her clothing—and concealed the water used for that purpose under the house. In support of that theory the State introduced a witness who testified that, being at the house on the Saturday following the killing—she saw some pigs come from under the house—with blood upon their noses. There was no objection made to this evidence at the time it was received, but on the next day the prisoner moved the court to strike it out as being irrelevant, which motion was refused. The evidence strikes us as being both pertinent and material. But conceding it to be as insisted upon for the defense, it was received without objection, and its reception cannot therefore be a just ground for exception. As for his Honor's refusal to strike it out on the next day when asked, we much doubt the legal propriety of such a course. Inadmissible evidence, unless objected to or forbidden by some positive law, may become competent evidence, so that the party offering it may acquire a right to it as such. But whether so or not (and we do not. mean to determine the point) the motion to strike out the evidence thus received without objection was certainly a matter addressed to the discretion of the Judge, the exercise of which we have no power to review.

As before stated, we find nothing in the case of which the prisoner can justly complain. He was tried by a jury fairly selected, and the law governing his case rightly administered.

Affirmed.

Cited. S. v. Spier 7 '86 N.C., 602; *S. v. Smith; ib.*7 707; *S. v. Burgwyn,* 87 N.C.,*573; S. v. Lawhorn,* 88 N. C., 637;: *S. v. Pratt ib.,* 641; *S. v. Suggs,* 89 N. C., 529; *Wilcoxon v. Logan,* 91 N.C., 451; *S. v. Davis,* 92 N. C., 767; *Branton v. 0'Briant,* 93 N.C., 104; *Jones v. Call, ib.* 179; *Smith v. Kron,* 96 N.C., 396; *S. v. Ellis,* 97 N.C., 449; *S. v.Crowson,* 98 N. C., 598; *S. v. Thomas ib.,* 602; *Leak v. Covington,* 99 N. C.,564; *Dugger v. McKesson,* 100 N. C. 6; *Johnson v. Allen, ib.* 136; *S. v. Johnsan, ib.* 495; *Fau con v. J ohnston,* 102 N. C., 269; *S. v. Whitfield,* 109 N. C., 878; *Simpson v. Pegram,* 112 N. C., 546; *Blue v: R.R.,* 117 N. C., 647; *S. v. Goff, ib.,* 761; *S. v: Spurling,* 118 N. C., 1252; *S. v. Traylor,* 121 N. C., 676; *S. v. Simpson,* 133 N.C., 678.

ORDER OF EXECUTION

State of North Carolina} Superior Court
McDowell County} Spring Term A.D. 1882

State}
Against}   Murder
Stephen Effler}

Judgment of the Court that the said Stephen Efler [sic] be remanded to the custody of the Sheriff of McDowell County to be kept by him safely and confined in the jail of said County until Friday the 19th day of May 1882, on which day between the Hours of Eleven O'clock A.M. and Two O'Clock P.M., he take the said Stephen Efler from said Jail and hang him by the neck until he be dead.—May the Lord have mercy upon his soul.

[seal]

A true copy, Given under my
hand an seal at office in Marion
this 19th day of May 1882.
D.O.H. W. Gillespie
Clerk Superior Court McDowell County

VI. Descendants of Stephen and Margaret Effler

As with the Frankie Silver case, there was a babe in arms who was a helpless and innocent witness to the horrible crime of its parent's murder. Frankie Silver's daughter, Nancy, grew up to marry a successful farmer and raise an extended family of her own, although with the tragedy of her husband's death in the Civil War and the devastating hard times that followed the war.

The child of Steve and Margaret "Peggie" Effler was named Joseph W. Effler at birth, and that is how his name is recorded in the U.S. Census of 1880. He was apparently named for his maternal grandfather. By the time Steve Effler wrote his confession, the day before he was hanged, the child's name had been changed to Alfred Erwin Effler. No one in the family knows why the name was changed.

I had been told that Alfred Erwin Effler lived to maturity, married and moved to Old Fort, but I knew very little about his family until January 7, 2001. That is when I received an e-mail from Alfred's great granddaughter, Anita Collins Justice Wages. As with the descendants of the murderess Frankie Silver, there had been a great deal of uncomfortable feelings to overcome in researching her ancestors. After all, it cannot have been easy for them to talk about a father or grandfather or great grandfather who had murdered his wife, their own mother, grandmother, great grandmother.

But, the crimes of the past were no fault of the present generation. And there was nothing to be gained by ignoring the past and pretending the murder never took place. Anita Wages became interested in her family history in 1977. She wrote me, "My daughter was born in 1976, and as I was trying to complete the genealogy section of her baby book, I could not answer some of the questions. When I began researching, it became addictive and I have accumulated a lot of information on many lines of my family.

"I was born in 1948 to Boyce Lee and Thelma Coralou Effler Justice, in Marion, N.C. I have lived here all of my life. I married in 1968 to Donald Collins. My son was born in 1971 and my daughter in 1976. My husband died suddenly in 1992 at the age of 49. I remarried a couple of years later to James Wages. I am a Registered Nurse, but retired from nursing two years ago after many years. I am also an elementary school teacher. I am presently teaching 5th grade, which I enjoy. I am 52 years old and hope to work a few more years.

"My mother and father are both still living. My dad is 76 and in poor health and my mother is 69 and is doing well. My mother was the 16th child of 16 children born to Alfred Erwin Effler and his wife Mae Belle Hughes. Alfred Erwin Effler was born on April 28, 1880. He was the 8 month old baby they found next to his dead mother when Steve Effler led some of his relatives and neighbors to his house after he killed her. He claimed she had a 'hurting in the head.' In reality, she had asthma and that was probably why she was so 'easy to kill' as he stated. I have two great aunts who are still living who told me she had asthma. That was about 10 years ago. They can't remember anything now.

"Therefore, Steven Effler and wife Margaret Grindstaff Effler would have been my great grandparents. He is buried in the Rayfield [or Lee Field] cemetery in Busick, N.C. in Yancey County. I have searched all over Mitchell and Yancey Counties trying to find where Margaret Grindstaff Effler, his wife, was buried. The family always said her people took her to Red Hill and buried her away from the Efflers. I can't find any record of this, hopefully, one day I will. My great aunts didn't like to be questioned about this crime. They are almost 90 now, and as you know, this kind of thing wasn't discussed much in their day."

In fact, Anita Wages is one among 43 great grandchildren of Steve and Peggy Effler. She continues to work on completing the family history as far back and as far forward as she can. In 2004, she published a book on "The Descendants of Lorrance Effler." That same year, she and others in the family erected a tombstone on the site where Steve Effler was supposed to have been buried beside his grandparents. She continues to search for her great grandmother's grave.

The author is grateful to Anita Wages for providing the following information on her family history:

Descendants of Stephen G. and Margaret Effler

Generation No. 1

1. STEPHEN G.₁ EFFLER was born February 04, 1860 in Washington County, TN, and died May 19, 1882 in McDowell County, NC (hanged). He married MARGARET GRINDSTAFF March 30, 1879 in Yancey Co. NC, At the home of Joseph Grindstaff, daughter of JOSEPH GRINDSTAFF and MARTHA RECTOR. She was born 1859 in Yancey Co. NC, and died January 06, 1881 in McDowell County, NC.

Child of STEPHEN EFFLER and MARGARET GRINDSTAFF is:
2.   i. ALFRED ERWIN₂ EFFLER, b. April 28, 1880, Yancey Co. NC; d. February 15, 1941, Old Fort, NC, McDowell Co.

Generation No. 2

2. ALFRED ERWIN₂ EFFLER *(STEPHEN G.₁)* was born April 28, 1880 in Yancey Co. NC, and died February 15, 1941 in Old Fort, NC, McDowell Co. He married MAEBELLE HUGHES May 24, 1905 in Marion, NC, McDowell Co., daughter of SAMUEL HUGHES and SARAH SHEHAN. She was born March 25, 1890 in?Yancey Co. NC, and died April 05, 1965 in Asheville, NC hospital; Buncombe Co. NC. ALFRED ERWIN EFFLER Was hit & killed by a car as he was walking along Hwy 70 in Old Fort, on 2/15/1941. Both are buried at Cherry Springs Cemetery

Children of ALFRED EFFLER and MAEBELLE HUGHES are:
      i. AGNES₃ EFFLER, b. January 19, 1906, Yancey Co. NC; d. February 14, 1906, Yancey Co. NC; buried Johnson Cem. Hwy 80 McDowell NC.
      ii. ROSEVELT EFFLER, b. May 26, 1907, Yancey Co. NC; d. May 26, 1907, Yancey Co. NC; buried Johnson Cem. Hwy 80 McDowell NC.
3.   iii. GEORGE ADAM EFFLER, b. July 29, 1908, McDowell Co. NC; d. November 16, 1978, Mitchell County, NC; buried Liberty FW Bapt.Cem.Marion,NC.
      iv. HORACE CLAYTON EFFLER, b. March 03, 1910, McDowell Co. NC; d. September 08, 1983, McDowell Co. NC; m. (1) EULA; m. (2) NANNIE B. ALLISON; b. April 13, 1899; d. June 18, 1957.
      v. ARNEL EFFLER, b. December 06, 1912, yancey Co. NC; d. December 07, 1912, Yancey Co. NC;buried Johnson Cem. Hwy 80 McDowell NC.
4.   vi. SAMUEL OLIVER EFFLER, b. November 19, 1913, McDowell Co. NC; d. December 31, 1975, Lexington, NC.
5.   vii. JAMES LEROY EFFLER, b. June 13, 1914, Yancey Co. NC; d. August 03, 1999, Buncombe County, NC.
6.   viii. MARGARET REBECCA EFFLER, b. November 01, 1915, McDowell Co.NC.
7.   ix. IOLA ELIZABETH EFFLER, b. April 07, 1918, Yancey Co. NC.

8.   x. WILLIAM LESTER EFFLER, b. December 18, 1920, Yancey Co. NC; d. May 31, 1998, Buncombe Co. NC.
9.   xi. LEWIS EDWARD EFFLER, b. April 05, 1922, Yancey Co. NC; d. May 17, 1998, McDowell Co. NC.
     xii. MYRTLE S. EFFLER, b. October 18, 1923, Yancey Co. NC; d. February 01, 1924, Yancey Co. NC; buried at Leefield Cemetery, Yancey Co. NC.
10. xiii. CALVIN FLOYD EFFLER, b. July 13, 1925, Yancey Co. NC; d. July 16, 2002, Buncombe Co. NC.
11. xiv. THOMAS ALVOID EFFLER, b. June 04, 1927, Yancey Co. NC; d. May 29, 1999, McDowell Co. NC; buried Cherry Springs Bapt. Old Fort, NC.
12. xv. ELVIE GARNET EFFLER, b. October 06, 1929, Yancey Co. NC.
13. xvi. THELMA CORALOU EFFLER, b. June 10, 1931, Yancey Co. NC.

Generation No. 3

3. GEORGE ADAM$_3$ EFFLER *(ALFRED ERWIN$_2$, STEPHEN G.$_1$)* was born July 29, 1908 in McDowell Co. NC, anddied November 16, 1978 in Mitchell County, NC; buried Liberty FW Bapt.Cem.Marion,NC. He married (1) FLORENCE THESODIA SHUFORD September 24, 1926 in Yancey Co. NC, daughter of DANIEL SHUFORD and MALINDA SHUFORD. She was born November 06, 1909, and died July 1974 in buried at Liberty FW Baptist Church, Marion, NC. He married (2) MOZELLE LEE April 18, 1975 in McDowell County, NC. She was born 1915.

Children of GEORGE EFFLER and FLORENCE SHUFORD are:
14. i. JAMES DANIEL$_4$ EFFLER, b. June 17, 1927.
15. ii. FRANCIS EARLY EFFLER, b. November 17, 1930.
16. iii. EVA ANGELINE (ANGIE) EFFLER, b. December 06, 1933; d. 1980.
17. iv. FREDA SAVANNA EFFLER, b. July 20, 1939.
18. v. WILLIAM PAUL EFFLER, b. June 08, 1941.
19. vi. HELEN ELAINE EFFLER, b. May 13, 1944.
20. vii. FRANKLIN DEAN EFFLER, b. April 19, 1946.
21. viii. JEWELL MARIE EFFLER, b. July 27, 1947.
22. ix. VERDIE VIOLA EFFLER, b. October 28, 1949.
23. x. WANDA BELLE EFFLER, b. September 06, 1954.

4. SAMUEL OLIVER$_3$ EFFLER *(ALFRED ERWIN$_2$, STEPHEN G.$_1$)* was born November 19, 1913 in McDowell Co. NC, and died December 31, 1975 in Lexington, NC. He married (1) ANNIE HOYLE. He married (2) BESSIE MAE CALLOWAY October 28, 1938 in Yancey Co. NC. She was born January 03, 1921, and died March 12, 1999 in Ashlawn Gardens, between Asheville & Weaverville, NC.

Children of SAMUEL EFFLER and BESSIE CALLOWAY are:
24. i. THELMA MARIE$_4$ EFFLER, b. July 25, 1939.
25. ii. RUBY JOE EFFLER, b. July 15, 1941.

26.   iii. EDWARD ROY LEE EFFLER, b. April 08, 1945.
27.   iv. PATRICIA ANN EFFLER, b. June 25, 1947.
28.   v. HAROLD EUGENE EFFLER, b. August 27, 1949; d. April 04, 1989, buried Living Waters Tabernacle Cem., McDowell Co NC.
      vi. NORMA PRICILLA EFFLER, b. February 10, 1951, McDowell Co. NC; d. September 17, 1955, McDowell Co. NC; buried Piney Grove Cem. Old Fort, NC.

5. JAMES LEROY₃ EFFLER *(ALFRED ERWIN₂, STEPHEN G.₁)* was born June 13, 1914 in Yancey Co. NC, and died August 03, 1999 in Buncombe County, NC. He married BERTHA ALLISON March 25, 1936 in Spartanburg, SC, daughter of NANNIE B. ALLISON. She was born December 01, 1919 in McDowell Co. NC.

Children of JAMES EFFLER and BERTHA ALLISON are:
      i. SHIRLEY JEAN₄ EFFLER, b. May 19, 1937, McDowell Co. NC; m. (1) ROBERT C. TURNER, May 11, 1956, Newport News, VA; b. Newport News, VA; d. July 08, 1977; m. (2) FRED J. VERNON, December 27, 1983, Yuma, Arizona; b. November 30, 1940, San Diego, California.
29.   ii. JOYCE ERLEAN EFFLER, b. May 28, 1938.
30.   iii. WILLIAM HOWARD EFFLER, b. June 03, 1940.
31.   iv. DONALD LEE EFFLER, b. May 16, 1944.

6. MARGARET REBECCA₃ EFFLER *(ALFRED ERWIN₂, STEPHEN G.₁)* was born November 01, 1915 in McDowell Co.NC. She married CHARLES EUGENE CARR September 30, 1940 in McDowell County, NC, son of ALFRED CARR and JESSIE KELLY. He was born November 05, 1915 in McDowell Co. NC, and died January 12, 1974 in NC.

Children of MARGARET EFFLER and CHARLES CARR are:
32.   i. CHARLES L.₄ CARR, b. April 22, 1939, McDowell Co. NC; d. September 07, 1995, buried Bethlehem Cem. McDowell Co. NC.
33.   ii. DORIS JEAN CARR, b. February 24, 1941, McDowell Co. NC.
34.   iii. TOMMY EDWARD CARR, b. May 04, 1942, McDowell Co. NC; d. June 29, 1994, McDowell Co. NC.

7. IOLA ELIZABETH₃ EFFLER *(ALFRED ERWIN₂, STEPHEN G.₁)* was born April 07, 1918 in Yancey Co. NC. She married (1) JOHN ALFRED CARR October 14, 1938 in McDowell County, NC, son of ALFRED CARR and JESSIE KELLY. He was born January 12, 1912, and died in died in World War II. She married (2) ROBERT MACK CARR November 06, 1947 in Yancey Co. NC, son of ALFRED CARR and JESSIE KELLY. He was born April 02, 1908 in McDowell Co. NC, and died February 19, 1998 in buried Bethlehem Cem. McDowell Co. NC.

Children of IOLA EFFLER and JOHN CARR are:
35.   i. RENA MAE₄ CARR, b. May 24, 1939.
36.   ii. MARY FRANCIS CARR, b. August 11, 1940.

8. WILLIAM LESTER$_3$ EFFLER *(ALFRED ERWIN$_2$, STEPHEN G.$_1$)* was born December 18, 1920 in Yancey Co. NC, and died May 31, 1998 in Buncombe Co. NC. He married (1) JOSEPHINE MARSH Abt. 1941, daughter of JOE MARSH and HARTLEY GRINDSTAFF. She was born June 19, 1924 in McDowell Co. NC, and died August 17, 1984 in Illinois. He married (2) BEATRICE O'DEAR Abt. 1950. She was born 1929. He married (3) LILY BERNICE EFFLER Abt. 1964, daughter of JAMES EFFLER and GERTRUDE WHEELER. She was born February 24, 1937. He married (4) MARY HELEN GIBSON Abt. 1973. She was born November 22, 1937 in Murphy, NC.

Child of WILLIAM EFFLER and JOSEPHINE MARSH is:
37.   i. ROBERT WAYNE$_4$ EFFLER, b. March 17, 1942, Marion, McDowell Co. NC.

Children of WILLIAM EFFLER and MARY GIBSON are:
38.   ii. KAREN DENISE$_4$ EFFLER, b. January 06, 1974.
39.   iii. WILLIAM EDWARD EFFLER, b. September 21, 1975, Buncombe, NC.

9. LEWIS EDWARD$_3$ EFFLER *(ALFRED ERWIN$_2$, STEPHEN G.$_1$)* was born April 05, 1922 in Yancey Co. NC, and died May 17, 1998 in McDowell Co. NC. He married RUBY DAVIS November 30, 1942, daughter of VIRGIL DAVIS and ETHEL MASON. She was born November 01, 1922 in McDowell Co. NC, and died April 11, 2002 in McDowell Co. NC.

Children of LEWIS EFFLER and RUBY DAVIS are:
40.   i. JOHN LOUIS$_4$ EFFLER, b. September 14, 1943.
41.   ii. JOYCE ANNETTE EFFLER, b. May 04, 1947.
42.   iii. ALFRED EUGENE "GENE" EFFLER, b. February 11, 1950.

10. CALVIN FLOYD$_3$ EFFLER *(ALFRED ERWIN$_2$, STEPHEN G.$_1$)* was born July 13, 1925 in Yancey Co. NC, and died July 16, 2002 in Buncombe Co. NC. He married MARY LOU FERGUSON April 23, 1949 in McDowell County, NC, daughter of ARVIN FERGUSON and MAGGIE JUSTICE. She was born April 04, 1924 in McDowell Co. NC, and died May 12, 1981 in Winston Salem, NC.

Children of CALVIN EFFLER and MARY FERGUSON are:
43.   i. WILLIAM CHARLES$_4$ EFFLER, b. March 01, 1950, Marion, McDowell Co. NC.
44.   ii. STEVEN FLOYD EFFLER, b. May 13, 1951, McDowell Co.NC.
45.   iii. KATHY DELORES EFFLER, b. December 19, 1960, McDowell Co. NC; d. November 12, 2004, Buncombe County, NC.

11. THOMAS ALVOID$_3$ EFFLER *(ALFRED ERWIN$_2$, STEPHEN G.$_1$)* was born June 04, 1927 in Yancey Co. NC, and died May 29, 1999 in McDowell Co. NC; buried Cherry Springs Bapt. Old Fort, NC. He married HELEN HANEY December 31, 1946 in McDowell

County, NC. She was born November 07, 1929 in McDowell Co. NC, and died April 27, 1979 in McDowell Co. NC; buried Cherry Springs Bapt. Old Fort, NC.

Children of THOMAS EFFLER and HELEN HANEY are:
46.   i. AGNES LOUISE$_4$ EFFLER, b. December 02, 1947.
47.   ii. JUNE ELIZABETH EFFLER, b. June 05, 1949.
48.   iii. THOMAS EDWARD EFFLER, b. November 03, 1950.
49.   iv. ROGER GLENN EFFLER, b. July 21, 1952, McDowell Co. NC.

12. ELVIE GARNET$_3$ EFFLER *(ALFRED ERWIN$_2$, STEPHEN G.$_1$)* was born October 06, 1929 in Yancey Co. NC. She married WILLARD LOWERY November 05, 1948 in Burke Co. NC. He was born January 16, 1925 in Wake County, NC, and died April 1971 in Wake County, Raleigh, NC.

Children of ELVIE EFFLER and WILLARD LOWERY are:
50.   i. TERRY GLENN$_4$ LOWERY, b. October 14, 1949.
51.   ii. RONALD WILLARD (RONNIE) LOWERY, b. April 07, 1951.
     iii. DWIGHT WAYNE LOWERY, b. June 16, 1956; m. MARCIA BARBOUR.
     iv. SHARON YVONNE LOWERY, b. May 11, 1958; m. EDWARD JONES.

13. THELMA CORALOU$_3$ EFFLER *(ALFRED ERWIN$_2$, STEPHEN G.$_1$)* was born June 10, 1931 in Yancey Co. NC. She married ROYCE JUSTICE June 27, 1947 in Marion, NC, McDowell Co. He was born May 05, 1924 in Fannin County, Georgia, and died June 12, 2001 in Marion, McDowell Co. NC.

Children of THELMA EFFLER and ROYCE JUSTICE are:
52.   i. SANDRA ANITA$_4$ JUSTICE, b. August 16, 1948, Marion, McDowell Co. NC.
     ii. VICKI EVANGELINE JUSTICE, b. March 01, 1950, Marion, McDowell Co. NC; m. JAMES D. TOTHEROW, Charleston, SC; b. 1948, Asheville, NC.
53.   iii. DONNA KAYE JUSTICE, b. August 31, 1951, McDowell Co. NC, Marion, NC.

Generation No. 4

14. JAMES DANIEL$_4$ EFFLER *(GEORGE ADAM$_3$, ALFRED ERWIN$_2$, STEPHEN G.$_1$)* was born June 17, 1927. He married (1) VIOLET JEAN MCCORMICK, daughter of JOHN WILLIAM MCCORMICK. She was born October 05, 1932, and died May 02, 1990 in Marion, McDowell, NC. He married (2) FRANCIS CAROLYN PRATTER February 22, 1993 in McDowell County, NC by C.L. Lytle, Justice of the Peace.

Children of JAMES EFFLER and VIOLET MCCORMICK are:
54.   i. MITCHELL EUGENE$_5$ EFFLER, b. April 23, 1949.
55.   ii. DWIGHT MILLARD EFFLER, b. January 14, 1952.

56.   iii. ROBERT (BOBBY) MARSHALL EFFLER, b. December 26, 1955.
57.   iv. JEFFREY KEITH EFFLER, b. March 29, 1961.

15. FRANCIS EARLY₄ EFFLER *(GEORGE ADAM₃, ALFRED ERWIN₂, STEPHEN G.₁)* was born November 17, 1930. She married UYETTE DAVIS March 10, 1947 in by J.L. Nichols, JP. He was born 1918.

Children of FRANCIS EFFLER and UYETTE DAVIS are:
58.   i. MERRILL LANE₅ DAVIS, b. January 04, 1950.
59.   ii. GLENDA RENA DAVIS, b. June 30, 1952.
60.   iii. MARTHA CAROL DAVIS, b. January 30, 1954.

16. EVA ANGELINE (ANGIE)₄ EFFLER *(GEORGE ADAM₃, ALFRED ERWIN₂, STEPHEN G.₁)* was born December 06, 1933, and died 1980. She married (1) BURLIN BARTLETT May 30, 1950 in wit: Rebecca Bartlett. He was born 1931. She married (2) GROVER WILLIAM HENSLEY Aft. 1960. He was born 1945.

Children of EVA EFFLER and BURLIN BARTLETT are:
61.   i. JUDY REVONDA₅ BARTLETT, b. December 04, 1953.
62.   ii. AUDIE LYNN BARTLETT, b. February 06, 1959.

17. FREDA SAVANNA₄ EFFLER *(GEORGE ADAM₃, ALFRED ERWIN₂, STEPHEN G.₁)* was born July 20, 1939. She married (1) VIRGIL BARTLETT. She married (2) TOM VANSTEENBERG.

Child of FREDA EFFLER and VIRGIL BARTLETT is:
63.   i. RICKY ALLAN₅ BARTLETT, b. December 29, 1964.

18. WILLIAM PAUL₄ EFFLER *(GEORGE ADAM₃, ALFRED ERWIN₂, STEPHEN G.₁)* was born June 08, 1941. He married (1) BETTY LOUVELL Abt. 1961. He married (2) MAGGIE ANN MATHIS Abt. 1972. She was born 1956.

Child of WILLIAM EFFLER and BETTY LOUVELL is:
      i. JAMES DONALD (DONNIE)₅ EFFLER, b. March 29, 1962.

Children of WILLIAM EFFLER and MAGGIE MATHIS are:
64.   ii. AMY GEORGETTE₅ EFFLER, b. August 30, 1973.
      iii. TIMOTHY PAUL EFFLER, b. September 17, 1981.

19. HELEN ELAINE₄ EFFLER *(GEORGE ADAM₃, ALFRED ERWIN₂, STEPHEN G.₁)* was born May 13, 1944. She married STOY ANTHONY JR. LANKFORD June 04, 1962. He was born March 25, 1945.

Children of HELEN EFFLER and STOY LANKFORD are:
65.   i. SCOTT DEAN$_5$ LANKFORD, b. May 21, 1963.
66.   ii. TODD LAMAR LANKFORD, b. February 15, 1966.
67.   iii. STEWARD PAUL LANKFORD, b. March 04, 1970.

20. FRANKLIN DEAN$_4$ EFFLER *(GEORGE ADAM$_3$, ALFRED ERWIN$_2$, STEPHEN G.$_1$)* was born April 19, 1946.

Children of FRANKLIN DEAN EFFLER are:
68.   i. WENDY YVETTE$_5$ EFFLER, b. July 09, 1971.
69.   ii. SUSAN KATHELEEN EFFLER, b. August 12, 1976.
      iii. KATHY JEANETTE EFFLER, b. November 09, 1980; m. SHAWN.

21. JEWELL MARIE$_4$ EFFLER *(GEORGE ADAM$_3$, ALFRED ERWIN$_2$, STEPHEN G.$_1$)* was born July 27, 1947. She married (1) DAVID LEE DULA November 06, 1970 in McDowell County, NC. He was born 1950 in Lenoir, NC. She married (2) MAURICE KING Aft. 1980.

Children of JEWELL EFFLER and DAVID DULA are:
70.   i. AARON VINCENT$_5$ DULA, b. July 11, 1971.
71.   ii. DAVIDA ELAINE DULA, b. July 02, 1979.

22. VERDIE VIOLA$_4$ EFFLER *(GEORGE ADAM$_3$, ALFRED ERWIN$_2$, STEPHEN G.$_1$)* was born October 28, 1949. She married (1) TERRY WILLIAMS. She married (2) ESTON "DUGGIE" CRAIG. She married (3) EDDIE BOYDEN GRANCUM October 17, 1969 in McDowell County, NC. He was born 1951.

Children of VERDIE EFFLER and TERRY WILLIAMS are:
72.   i. AMBREA DAWN$_5$ WILLIAMS, b. May 11, 1970.
73.   ii. JOSEPH MICHEL (JOE) WILLIAMS, b. November 06, 1973.
74.   iii. KIMBERLY HOPE WILLIAMS, b. January 14, 1975.

23. WANDA BELLE$_4$ EFFLER *(GEORGE ADAM$_3$, ALFRED ERWIN$_2$, STEPHEN G.$_1$)* was born September 06, 1954. She married (1) FRED RUSSELL JR. HARRIS June 09, 1972 in McDowell County, NC. He was born 1952. She married (2) CLARK WALL Aft. 1979.

Children of WANDA EFFLER and FRED HARRIS are:
75.   i. SHERRILL DERRICK (BO)$_5$ HARRIS, b. December 16, 1972.
76.   ii. SHAUN RUSSELL HARRIS, b. February 13, 1978.

24. THELMA MARIE$_4$ EFFLER *(SAMUEL OLIVER$_3$, ALFRED ERWIN$_2$, STEPHEN G.$_1$)* was born July 25, 1939. She met (2) JAMES BROWN Abt. 1958. She married (3) BUDDY RICARDO BLANKENSHIP Abt. 1960. She married (4) JERRY P. BEST Aft. 1990.

Children of THELMA MARIE EFFLER are:
77. i. LEONARD (BUDDY)₅ EFFLER, b. November 28, 1954.
78. ii. HOWARD EDWARD EFFLER, b. December 29, 1956; d. March 01, 1987.

Child of THELMA EFFLER and JAMES BROWN is:
iii. LINDA JO₅ EFFLER, b. February 14, 1959; d. April 09, 1959.

Child of THELMA EFFLER and BUDDY BLANKENSHIP is:
79. iv. RICARDO EUGENE (RICKEY)₅ BLANKENSHIP, b. November 08, 1960; d. December 04, 1982.

25. RUBY JOE₄ EFFLER *(SAMUEL OLIVER₃, ALFRED ERWIN₂, STEPHEN G.₁)* was born July 15, 1941. She married JAMES DANIEL JR. ROBERSON.

Children of RUBY EFFLER and JAMES ROBERSON are:
80. i. PAMELA ANNETTE₅ ROBERSON, b. June 19, 1963.
81. ii. JAMES BRIAN ROBERSON, b. November 09, 1969.

26. EDWARD ROY LEE₄ EFFLER *(SAMUEL OLIVER₃, ALFRED ERWIN₂, STEPHEN G.₁)* was born April 08, 1945. He married LINDA BISHOP. She was born 1950.

Children of EDWARD EFFLER and LINDA BISHOP are:
i. NORMA DIANE₅ EFFLER, b. January 14, 1972.
82. ii. SAMUEL "BO" EDWARD EFFLER, b. May 21, 1973.

27. PATRICIA ANN₄ EFFLER *(SAMUEL OLIVER₃, ALFRED ERWIN₂, STEPHEN G.₁)* was born June 25, 1947. She married ALVIN W. FULLER.

Child of PATRICIA EFFLER and ALVIN FULLER is:
i. DUSTIN₅ FULLER, b. October 14, 1985.

28. HAROLD EUGENE₄ EFFLER *(SAMUEL OLIVER₃, ALFRED ERWIN₂, STEPHEN G.₁)* was born August 27, 1949, and died April 04, 1989 in buried Living Waters Tabernacle Cem., McDowell Co NC. He married (1) CAROL ANN. He married (2) SANDRA HENSLEY. She was born Abt. 1950.

Children of HAROLD EFFLER and CAROL ANN are:
i. MICHAEL EUGENE₅ EFFLER, b. January 26, 1973.
ii. DANIEL EFFLER.

Child of HAROLD EFFLER and SANDRA HENSLEY is:
iii. DAVID JAMIE₅ EFFLER, b. December 15, 1981.

Child of HAROLD EUGENE EFFLER is:
iv. KEVIN₅ EFFLER.

29. JOYCE ERLEAN₄ EFFLER *(JAMES LEROY₃, ALFRED ERWIN₂, STEPHEN G.₁)* was born May 28, 1938. She married (1) PAUL SHELTON May 28, 1957 in Lancaster, SC. He was born November 29, 1928 in Erwin, Tennessee, and died May 09, 1985 in Hampton, VA. She married (2) WILLIAM R. (BILL) JONES September 02, 1992 in McDowell County, NC. He was born May 23, 1943 in Sylva, NC.

Child of JOYCE EFFLER and PAUL SHELTON is:
i. ROBERT EUGENE (ROBBIE)₅ SHELTON, b. September 25, 1960, born in VA; lives in Long Beach, California.

30. WILLIAM HOWARD₄ EFFLER *(JAMES LEROY₃, ALFRED ERWIN₂, STEPHEN G.₁)* was born June 03, 1940. He married ANNA DEAN "DEANNIE" EVANS October 22, 1956 in Roanoke, VA. She was born October 22, 1940.

Children of WILLIAM EFFLER and ANNA EVANS are:
i. KENNETH LEE₅ EFFLER, b. April 30, 1957, Williamsburg, VA; d. August 21, 1976, Newport News, VA.
83. ii. HOWARD DWAYNE EFFLER, b. November 11, 1961, Newport News, VA.

31. DONALD LEE₄ EFFLER *(JAMES LEROY₃, ALFRED ERWIN₂, STEPHEN G.₁)* was born May 16, 1944. He married JANET MARIE HARRIS May 30, 1964 in Newport News, VA. She was born January 19, 1945 in Shelby, NC.

Children of DONALD EFFLER and JANET HARRIS are:
i. RHONDA MARIE₅ EFFLER, b. October 25, 1970, Newport News, VA; m. (1) RONALD WAYNE BROWN, August 28, 1993, McDowell County, NC; b. January 10, 1956, McDowell Co. NC; d. November 27, 1996, Buncombe County, NC; m. (2) MICHAEL PERRY MOORE, June 30, 2000, McDowell County, NC; b. August 13, 1963, McDowell Co. NC.
84. ii. DONITA LYNN EFFLER, b. January 25, 1975, Newport News, VA.

32. CHARLES L.₄ CARR *(MARGARET REBECCA₃ EFFLER, ALFRED ERWIN₂, STEPHEN G.₁)* was born April 22, 1939 in McDowell Co. NC, and died September 07, 1995 in buried Bethlehem Cem. McDowell Co. NC. He married LINDA DALORESTHOMAS, daughter of ALBERT "BUD" THOMAS. She was born September 17, 1945.

Child of CHARLES CARR and LINDA DALORESTHOMAS is:
i. LISA₅ CARR, m. MALE HAYNES.

33. DORIS JEAN$_4$ CARR *(MARGARET REBECCA$_3$ EFFLER, ALFRED ERWIN$_2$, STEPHEN G.$_1$)* was born February 24, 1941 in McDowell Co. NC. She married (1) WAYNE GUDGAR LYTLE December 28, 1961 in McDowell County, NC, son of GUDGAR LYTLE and MARY BURGIN. He was born December 08, 1939 in McDowell Co. NC, and died January 28, 1967 in McDowell Co. NC. She married (2) HAROLD HENSLEY Abt. 1969. He was born August 06, 1940.

Child of DORIS CARR and WAYNE LYTLE is:
    i. JEFFREY WAYNE$_5$ LYTLE, b. March 08, 1962.

Child of DORIS CARR and HAROLD HENSLEY is:
85.   ii. REGINA LYNN$_5$ HENSLEY, b. January 31, 1971.

34. TOMMY EDWARD$_4$ CARR *(MARGARET REBECCA$_3$ EFFLER, ALFRED ERWIN$_2$, STEPHEN G.$_1$)* was born May 04, 1942 in McDowell Co. NC, and died June 29, 1994 in McDowell Co. NC. He married (1) EDNA JO FOWLER February 07, 1961 in McDowell County, NC. She was born 1944. He married (2) ANN BRADLEY Abt. 1964. She was born Abt. 1946.

Children of TOMMY CARR and ANN BRADLEY are:
86.   i. MICHAEL EDWARD$_5$ CARR, b. February 07, 1964.
    ii. MITCHELL CARR.
    iii. MATTHEW CARR.

35. RENA MAE$_4$ CARR *(IOLA ELIZABETH$_3$ EFFLER, ALFRED ERWIN$_2$, STEPHEN G.$_1$)* was born May 24, 1939. She married (1) WILLIAM LAWSON Abt. 1956. He was born Abt. 1937. She married (2) MALE HALL Abt. 1990. He died Abt. 2003.

Children of RENA CARR and WILLIAM LAWSON are:
87.   i. TONY LEE$_5$ LAWSON, b. November 29, 1957.
88.   ii. VICKI RENEE LAWSON, b. August 09, 1959.
89.   iii. WILLIAM SCOTT LAWSON, b. October 10, 1962.

36. MARY FRANCIS$_4$ CARR *(IOLA ELIZABETH$_3$ EFFLER, ALFRED ERWIN$_2$, STEPHEN G.$_1$)* was born August 11, 1940. She married HARRY BURGIN LYTLE October 15, 1960, son of GUDGER LYTLE. He was born January 10, 1938.

Children of MARY CARR and HARRY LYTLE are:
90.   i. HARRY RICHARD$_5$ LYTLE, b. September 22, 1961.
91.   ii. KIMBERLY JEANINE LYTLE, b. September 16, 1963.
92.   iii. KEVIN ROBERT LYTLE, b. March 28, 1974.

37. ROBERT WAYNE$_4$ EFFLER (*WILLIAM LESTER$_3$, ALFRED ERWIN$_2$, STEPHEN G.$_1$*) was born March 17, 1942 in Marion, McDowell Co. NC. He married JANE ANN HAMPTON.

Children of ROBERT EFFLER and JANE HAMPTON are:
93.   i. ROBERT DWAYNE$_5$ EFFLER, b. March 16, 1961.
94.   ii. LELANA LYNN EFFLER, b. September 24, 1962.
95.   iii. CHRISTIE JANE EFFLER, b. March 08, 1964.

38. KAREN DENISE$_4$ EFFLER (*WILLIAM LESTER$_3$, ALFRED ERWIN$_2$, STEPHEN G.$_1$*) was born January 06, 1974. She married DAVID PAUL BURRELL. He was born December 05, 1952.

Children of KAREN EFFLER and DAVID BURRELL are:
      i. CODY ALAN$_5$ BURRELL, b. March 19, 1994.
      ii. MARK PAUL BURRELL, b. November 28, 1998.

39. WILLIAM EDWARD$_4$ EFFLER (*WILLIAM LESTER$_3$, ALFRED ERWIN$_2$, STEPHEN G.$_1$*) was born September 21, 1975 in Buncombe, NC. He married (2) CHRISTIE Abt. 1993. He married (3) TRACY DAVIS Abt. 1997. She was born March 03, 1972.

Child of WILLIAM EDWARD EFFLER is:
      i. MICHAEL ISAIAH$_5$ EFFLER, b. September 25, 1997.

Child of WILLIAM EFFLER and CHRISTIE is:
      ii. CHRISTOPHER EDWARD$_5$ EFFLER, b. August 16, 1994.

Children of WILLIAM EFFLER and TRACY DAVIS are:
      iii. KAYLA ANN$_5$ EFFLER, b. May 06, 1997.
      iv. HUNTER LEE EFFLER, b. November 07, 1998.

40. JOHN LOUIS$_4$ EFFLER (*LEWIS EDWARD$_3$, ALFRED ERWIN$_2$, STEPHEN G.$_1$*) was born September 14, 1943. He married FREIDA GAIL BRYANT, daughter of JAMES BRYANT and ADA GRAGG.

Children of JOHN EFFLER and FREIDA BRYANT are:
96.   i. REBECCA LEIGH$_5$ EFFLER.
97.   ii. ANGELA GAIL EFFLER.

41. JOYCE ANNETTE$_4$ EFFLER (*LEWIS EDWARD$_3$, ALFRED ERWIN$_2$, STEPHEN G.$_1$*) was born May 04, 1947. She married CHARLES WILSON ANDERSON. He was born July 12, 1945.

Children of JOYCE EFFLER and CHARLES ANDERSON are:
  i. CHARLES ANTHONY (TINKER)₅ ANDERSON, b. March 25, 1962.
  ii. TINA JOYCE ANDERSON, b. November 13, 1963.
  iii. JENNY LEE ANDERSON, b. September 13, 1965.
  iv. SHANE D. ANDERSON, b. November 1966.

42. ALFRED EUGENE "GENE"₄ EFFLER *(LEWIS EDWARD₃, ALFRED ERWIN₂, STEPHEN G.₁)* was born February 11, 1950. He married (2) VIRGINIA R. RANDOLPH August 14, 1976 in McDowell County, NC. She was born October 27, 1955.

Child of ALFRED EUGENE "GENE" EFFLER is:
98.   i. MICHELLE LORENE₅ EFFLER, b. May 18, 1970.

Children of ALFRED EFFLER and VIRGINIA RANDOLPH are:
  ii. ADAM EUGENE₅ EFFLER, b. February 25, 1994.
  iii. SARAH GRACE EFFLER, b. November 21, 1995.
  iv. REBEKAH LEIGH EFFLER, b. November 21, 1995.

43. WILLIAM CHARLES₄ EFFLER *(CALVIN FLOYD₃, ALFRED ERWIN₂, STEPHEN G.₁)* was born March 01, 1950 in Marion, McDowell Co. NC. He married (1) JANE OGLE. He married (2) PAMELA DARLENE STRICKLAND July 26, 1997 in McDowell County, NC.

Children of WILLIAM EFFLER and JANE OGLE are:
  i. SHANE DOUGLAS₅ EFFLER, b. September 19, 1973.
  ii. BRENT EVAN EFFLER, b. June 05, 1975.
  iii. JESSICA NICOLE EFFLER, b. December 17, 1976.
99.   iv. MATTHEW CHARLES EFFLER, b. October 05, 1978.

44. STEVEN FLOYD₄ EFFLER *(CALVIN FLOYD₃, ALFRED ERWIN₂, STEPHEN G.₁)* was born May 13, 1951 in McDowell Co.NC. He married DONNA KAYE BARTLETT May 10, 1974 in McDowell County, NC. She was born 1954 in McDowell Co. NC.

Children of STEVEN EFFLER and DONNA BARTLETT are:
  i. JENNIFER MARIE₅ EFFLER, b. April 09, 1973.
  ii. JEREMY EFFLER, b. October 13, 1979.
  iii. MARY ELIZABETH EFFLER, b. March 02, 1984.

45. KATHY DELORES₄ EFFLER *(CALVIN FLOYD₃, ALFRED ERWIN₂, STEPHEN G.₁)* was born December 19, 1960 in McDowell Co. NC, and died November 12, 2004 in Buncombe County, NC. She married MARC LEVINE Abt. 1989 in Black Mountain, Buncombe Co. NC, son of JIM LEVINE and ANN MARIE.

Child of KATHY EFFLER and MARC LEVINE is:
    i. JOSH$_5$ LEVINE, b. March 01, 1994.

46. AGNES LOUISE$_4$ EFFLER *(THOMAS ALVOID$_3$, ALFRED ERWIN$_2$, STEPHEN G.$_1$)* was born December 02, 1947. She married ALBERT GLENN "BILL" BAILEY. He was born June 25, 1947.

Children of AGNES EFFLER and ALBERT BAILEY are:
100. i. KENNETH$_5$ BAILEY, b. February 07, 1970.
101. ii. KEVIN BAILEY, b. July 26, 1973.
102. iii. CHRISTINA DE ANN BAILEY, b. November 10, 1978.

47. JUNE ELIZABETH$_4$ EFFLER *(THOMAS ALVOID$_3$, ALFRED ERWIN$_2$, STEPHEN G.$_1$)* was born June 05, 1949. She married DONALD BRISCOE HILL, son of BRISCOE HILL and CARTHA. He was born July 23, 1948.

Children of JUNE EFFLER and DONALD HILL are:
    i. JOSEPH EUGENE$_5$ HILL, b. January 14, 1970.
103. ii. DONNA HILL, b. October 07, 1974.
    iii. MARK HILL, b. May 19, 1980.

48. THOMAS EDWARD$_4$ EFFLER *(THOMAS ALVOID$_3$, ALFRED ERWIN$_2$, STEPHEN G.$_1$)* was born November 03, 1950. He married SANDRA LYNN (SANDY) BROWN September 23, 1971 in McDowell County, NC. She was born September 21, 1953.

Children of THOMAS EFFLER and SANDRA BROWN are:
104. i. MICHELLE LYNN$_5$ EFFLER, b. June 17, 1975.
105. ii. JAMES WILLIAM (J.W.) EFFLER, b. September 22, 1977.
106. iii. MELISSA ANN EFFLER, b. December 01, 1980.

49. ROGER GLENN$_4$ EFFLER *(THOMAS ALVOID$_3$, ALFRED ERWIN$_2$, STEPHEN G.$_1$)* was born July 21, 1952 in McDowell Co. NC. He married SHERYL LYN WATSON. She was born January 14, 1953.

Children of ROGER EFFLER and SHERYL WATSON are:
    i. JENNIFER CAMILE$_5$ EFFLER, b. November 02, 1978.
    ii. CAROLINE ELIZABETH EFFLER, b. July 18, 1984.

50. TERRY GLENN$_4$ LOWERY *(ELVIE GARNET$_3$ EFFLER, ALFRED ERWIN$_2$, STEPHEN G.$_1$)* was born October 14, 1949. He married JEAN LOWERY. She was born February 04, 1949.

Children of TERRY LOWERY and JEAN LOWERY are:
    i. DAWN$_5$ LOWERY, b. September 10, 1969.
    ii. MICHELLE LOWERY, b. November 21, 1973.

51. RONALD WILLARD (RONNIE)$_4$ LOWERY (*ELVIE GARNET$_3$ EFFLER, ALFRED ERWIN$_2$, STEPHEN G.$_1$*) was born April 07, 1951. He married (1) ALENA LOWERY.

Children of RONALD WILLARD (RONNIE) LOWERY are:
107. i. RUSTY WILLARD$_5$ LOWERY, b. January 29, 1973.
108. ii. TOBY LOWERY, b. April 07, 1975.

52. SANDRA ANITA$_4$ JUSTICE (*THELMA CORALOU$_3$ EFFLER, ALFRED ERWIN$_2$, STEPHEN G.$_1$*) was born August 16, 1948 in Marion, McDowell Co. NC. She married (1) DONALD LEE COLLINS June 27, 1968 in Marion, NC, McDowell Co. E. Marion Bapt. Church, son of ROY COLLINS and MAUDE FRYE. He was born May 16, 1943 in Harlan County, Ky., and died July 04, 1992 in Marion, McDowell Co. NC. She married (2) JAMES (JIM) CRAIG WAGES June 05, 1993 in Marion, NC, McDowell Co.; New Manna Bapt. Church. He was born June 30, 1948 in Louisville, Jefferson County, Kentucky.

Children of SANDRA JUSTICE and DONALD COLLINS are:
109. i. DONALD LEE II$_5$ COLLINS, b. January 31, 1971, Morganton, Burke Co. NC.
     ii. BRIGETTE Y. COLLINS, b. July 26, 1976, Burke County, Morganton,NC; m. BRIAN SHIMBERG, April 27, 2002, Gatlinburg, TN; b. July 31, 1978.

53. DONNA KAYE$_4$ JUSTICE (*THELMA CORALOU$_3$ EFFLER, ALFRED ERWIN$_2$, STEPHEN G.$_1$*) was born August 31, 1951 in McDowell Co. NC, Marion, NC. She married (1) WAYNE FRANKLIN 1969 in Gaffney, SC, son of WINIFRED FRANKLIN and LONNIE. He was born 1951 in Morganton, Burke Co. NC. She married (2) DONNIE WALDOCH Abt. 1993. He was born 1952.

Child of DONNA JUSTICE and WAYNE FRANKLIN is:
110. i. TONYA LYNN$_5$ FRANKLIN, b. September 26, 1970, Morganton, NC.

Generation No. 5

54. MITCHELL EUGENE$_5$ EFFLER (*JAMES DANIEL$_4$, GEORGE ADAM$_3$, ALFRED ERWIN$_2$, STEPHEN G.$_1$*) was born April 23, 1949. He married PAM.

Children of MITCHELL EFFLER and PAM are:
111. i. CHRISTOPHER SCOTT$_6$ EFFLER, b. May 08, 1973.
112. ii. JASON BRIAN EFFLER, b. August 05, 1974.

55. DWIGHT MILLARD$_5$ EFFLER *(JAMES DANIEL$_4$, GEORGE ADAM$_3$, ALFRED ERWIN$_2$, STEPHEN G.$_1$)* was born January 14, 1952. He married GENELL MINNIE BEAN December 16, 1971 in McDowell County, NC.

Children of DWIGHT EFFLER and GENELL BEAN are:
    i. JEROME DANIEL$_6$ EFFLER, b. May 15, 1974.
113. ii. VERA LYNN EFFLER, b. July 07, 1977.
114. iii. JOSHUA DWIGHT EFFLER, b. June 11, 1984.

56. ROBERT (BOBBY) MARSHALL$_5$ EFFLER *(JAMES DANIEL$_4$, GEORGE ADAM$_3$, ALFRED ERWIN$_2$, STEPHEN G.$_1$)* was born December 26, 1955. He married SYLVIA JANELL HARRIS May 04, 1974 in McDowell County, NC. She was born 1958.

Children of ROBERT EFFLER and SYLVIA HARRIS are:
115. i. MALINDA LEIGH$_6$ EFFLER, b. February 18, 1977.
    ii. ROBERT (ROBBIE) MARSHALL JR. EFFLER, b. June 23, 1979; m. NOVA REBECCA HICKS, April 22, 2002, McDowell County, NC.

57. JEFFREY KEITH$_5$ EFFLER *(JAMES DANIEL$_4$, GEORGE ADAM$_3$, ALFRED ERWIN$_2$, STEPHEN G.$_1$)* was born March 29, 1961. He married MONICA SUZANNE BROOKS. She was born February 08, 1963.

Children of JEFFREY EFFLER and MONICA BROOKS are:
    i. ALLEN KEITH$_6$ EFFLER, b. September 30, 1981.
    ii. JEFFREY KENNETH "KENNY" EFFLER, b. March 18, 1988.

58. MERRILL LANE$_5$ DAVIS *(FRANCIS EARLY$_4$ EFFLER, GEORGE ADAM$_3$, ALFRED ERWIN$_2$, STEPHEN G.$_1$)* was born January 04, 1950. He married (1) SHIRLEY SWORD. He married (2) JANE.

Child of MERRILL DAVIS and SHIRLEY SWORD is:
116. i. DAVID LANE$_6$ DAVIS, b. September 07, 1974.

59. GLENDA RENA$_5$ DAVIS *(FRANCIS EARLY$_4$ EFFLER, GEORGE ADAM$_3$, ALFRED ERWIN$_2$, STEPHEN G.$_1$)* was born June 30, 1952. She married RONNIE (BUD) GODFREY.

Children of GLENDA DAVIS and RONNIE GODFREY are:
117. i. GARY LEE$_6$ GODFREY, b. March 15, 1972.
118. ii. MICHAEL LANE GODFREY, b. December 28, 1973.
119. iii. KIMBERLY LYNETTE GODFREY, b. February 26, 1977.
    iv. TOMMY BRISTON GODFREY, b. March 12, 1978.

60. MARTHA CAROL$_5$ DAVIS *(FRANCIS EARLY$_4$ EFFLER, GEORGE ADAM$_3$, ALFRED ERWIN$_2$, STEPHEN G.$_1$)* was born January 30, 1954. She married JAMES OLIVER LUNSFORD, son of CLAUDE LUNSFORD and DORIS EFFLER. He was born March 31, 1952.

Children of MARTHA DAVIS and JAMES LUNSFORD are:
120. i. MICHELLE RENA$_6$ LUNSFORD, b. September 13, 1972.
121. ii. MELISSA DAWN LUNSFORD, b. October 30, 1973.
122. iii. CHRISTOPHER CHAD LUNSFORD, b. July 18, 1977.

61. JUDY REVONDA$_5$ BARTLETT *(EVA ANGELINE (ANGIE)$_4$ EFFLER, GEORGE ADAM$_3$, ALFRED ERWIN$_2$, STEPHEN G.$_1$)* was born December 04, 1953. She married (1) DAVID HENSLEY. He was born Abt. 1951. She married (2) WAYNE MATHIS.

Children of JUDY BARTLETT and DAVID HENSLEY are:
123. i. RANDY KEITH$_6$ HENSLEY, b. October 08, 1968.
124. ii. PAMELA RENA HENSLEY, b. October 04, 1970.

Child of JUDY BARTLETT and WAYNE MATHIS is:
125. iii. JENNIFER LEIGH$_6$ MATHIS, b. September 09, 1981.

62. AUDIE LYNN$_5$ BARTLETT *(EVA ANGELINE (ANGIE)$_4$ EFFLER, GEORGE ADAM$_3$, ALFRED ERWIN$_2$, STEPHEN G.$_1$)* was born February 06, 1959.

Children of AUDIE LYNN BARTLETT are:
i. TAMMY MIRANDA$_6$ BARTLETT, b. May 24, 1979.
ii. TEESA LYNN BARTLETT, b. November 28, 1981.

63. RICKY ALLAN$_5$ BARTLETT *(FREDA SAVANNA$_4$ EFFLER, GEORGE ADAM$_3$, ALFRED ERWIN$_2$, STEPHEN G.$_1$)* was born December 29, 1964. He married KRISTIANA COLDTRAIN.

Children of RICKY BARTLETT and KRISTIANA COLDTRAIN are:
i. DOUGLAS ANTHONY$_6$ BARTLETT, b. September 09, 1987.
ii. BRANDY NICOLE BARTLETT, b. June 03, 1996.
iii. THOMAS MICHAEL BARTLETT, b. September 07, 2000.
iv. AMANDA RENEE BARTLETT, b. August 09, 2002.

64. AMY GEORGETTE$_5$ EFFLER *(WILLIAM PAUL$_4$, GEORGE ADAM$_3$, ALFRED ERWIN$_2$, STEPHEN G.$_1$)* was born August 30, 1973. She married TOMMY NATHANIEL PHILLIPS November 23, 1996 in McDowell County, NC.

Child of AMY EFFLER and TOMMY PHILLIPS is:
    i. TOMMY NATHANIEL II$_6$ PHILLIPS, b. November 17, 1999.

65. SCOTT DEAN$_5$ LANKFORD *(HELEN ELAINE$_4$ EFFLER, GEORGE ADAM$_3$, ALFRED ERWIN$_2$, STEPHEN G.$_1$)* was born May 21, 1963. He married SARAH.

Children of SCOTT LANKFORD and SARAH are:
    i. CHRISTOPHER SCOTT$_6$ LANKFORD, b. July 27, 1984.
    ii. DUSTIN TODD LANKFORD, b. December 24, 1985.

66. TODD LAMAR$_5$ LANKFORD *(HELEN ELAINE$_4$ EFFLER, GEORGE ADAM$_3$, ALFRED ERWIN$_2$, STEPHEN G.$_1$)* was born February 15, 1966. He married DONETTE.

Children of TODD LANKFORD and DONETTE are:
    i. LANDON TODD$_6$ LANKFORD, b. September 09, 1986.
    ii. CODY LAMAR LANKFORD, b. October 12, 1991.

67. STEWARD PAUL$_5$ LANKFORD *(HELEN ELAINE$_4$ EFFLER, GEORGE ADAM$_3$, ALFRED ERWIN$_2$, STEPHEN G.$_1$)* was born March 04, 1970. He married TONYA WHITE.

Child of STEWARD LANKFORD and TONYA WHITE is:
    i. MEGAN MICHELLE$_6$ LANKFORD, b. November 04, 1991.

68. WENDY YVETTE$_5$ EFFLER *(FRANKLIN DEAN$_4$, GEORGE ADAM$_3$, ALFRED ERWIN$_2$, STEPHEN G.$_1$)* was born July 09, 1971. She married MARK TESTER.

Children of WENDY EFFLER and MARK TESTER are:
    i. SAVANNAH BLAKE$_6$ TESTER, b. February 22, 1992.
    ii. TROY MARK TESTER, b. June 02, 1994.
    iii. FRANKLIN JAMES TESTER, b. December 29, 2002.

69. SUSAN KATHELEEN$_5$ EFFLER *(FRANKLIN DEAN$_4$, GEORGE ADAM$_3$, ALFRED ERWIN$_2$, STEPHEN G.$_1$)* was born August 12, 1976. She married JOEY ELLIOTT.

Child of SUSAN EFFLER and JOEY ELLIOTT is:
    i. ELIZABETH KAYLYNN$_6$ ELLIOTT, b. May 27, 2003.

70. AARON VINCENT$_5$ DULA *(JEWELL MARIE$_4$ EFFLER, GEORGE ADAM$_3$, ALFRED ERWIN$_2$, STEPHEN G.$_1$)* was born July 11, 1971. He married TINA PRICE.

Children of AARON DULA and TINA PRICE are:
    i. JACOB NEAL$_6$ DULA, b. March 18, 1991.
    ii. JOSHUA ADAM DULA, b. August 12, 1996.
    iii. JARRETT BRYON DULA, b. August 28, 1997.
    iv. ETHAN JEAN DULA, b. March 05, 1999.

71. DAVIDA ELAINE$_5$ DULA *(JEWELL MARIE$_4$ EFFLER, GEORGE ADAM$_3$, ALFRED ERWIN$_2$, STEPHEN G.$_1$)* was born July 02, 1979. She married JAMMIE KAYLOR.

Children of DAVIDA DULA and JAMMIE KAYLOR are:
    i. MICAH STORM$_6$ DULA, b. January 03, 1998.
    ii. ELAINA SKY KAYLOR, b. September 16, 2000.
    iii. JADA RAIN KAYLOR, b. March 26, 2002.

72. AMBREA DAWN$_5$ WILLIAMS *(VERDIE VIOLA$_4$ EFFLER, GEORGE ADAM$_3$, ALFRED ERWIN$_2$, STEPHEN G.$_1$)* was born May 11, 1970. She married DENNIS BYRD.

Child of AMBREA WILLIAMS and DENNIS BYRD is:
    i. MIRANDA DAWN$_6$ BYRD, b. March 05, 1991.

73. JOSEPH MICHEL (JOE)$_5$ WILLIAMS *(VERDIE VIOLA$_4$ EFFLER, GEORGE ADAM$_3$, ALFRED ERWIN$_2$, STEPHEN G.$_1$)* was born November 06, 1973. He married ANGELA.

Child of JOSEPH WILLIAMS and ANGELA is:
    i. ZEDRICK MICHAEL$_6$ WILLIAMS, b. March 30, 1998.

74. KIMBERLY HOPE$_5$ WILLIAMS *(VERDIE VIOLA$_4$ EFFLER, GEORGE ADAM$_3$, ALFRED ERWIN$_2$, STEPHEN G.$_1$)* was born January 14, 1975. She married MALE RICH.

Child of KIMBERLY WILLIAMS and MALE RICH is:
    i. COLTON VENOY$_6$ RICH, b. May 08, 1999.

75. SHERRILL DERRICK (BO)$_5$ HARRIS *(WANDA BELLE$_4$ EFFLER, GEORGE ADAM$_3$, ALFRED ERWIN$_2$, STEPHEN G.$_1$)* was born December 16, 1972.

Children of SHERRILL DERRICK (BO) HARRIS are:
    i. SAMANTHA ALEXANDRIA$_6$ HARRIS, b. May 31, 1989.
    ii. CHASITY NICOLE HARRIS, b. August 20, 1997.
    iii. REAGAN ANN-MARIE HARRIS, b. January 14, 2002.

76. SHAUN RUSSELL$_5$ HARRIS (*WANDA BELLE$_4$ EFFLER, GEORGE ADAM$_3$, ALFRED ERWIN$_2$, STEPHEN G.$_1$*) was born February 13, 1978.

Child of SHAUN RUSSELL HARRIS is:
    i. CARRINGTON RACHEL$_6$ HARRIS, b. April 06, 1998.

77. LEONARD (BUDDY)$_5$ EFFLER (*THELMA MARIE$_4$, SAMUEL OLIVER$_3$, ALFRED ERWIN$_2$, STEPHEN G.$_1$*) was born November 28, 1954. He married TAMMY ROSE FOX.

Children of LEONARD EFFLER and TAMMY FOX are:
126. i. LEONARD DOUGLAS$_6$ EFFLER, b. March 08, 1974.
127. ii. JASON DANIEL EFFLER, b. November 08, 1978.
    iii. BRANDON COLE EFFLER, b. August 29, 1983.
    iv. TAMMY NICOLE EFFLER, b. July 05, 1986.

78. HOWARD EDWARD$_5$ EFFLER (*THELMA MARIE$_4$, SAMUEL OLIVER$_3$, ALFRED ERWIN$_2$, STEPHEN G.$_1$*) was born December 29, 1956, and died March 01, 1987. He married (1) DEBRA DARLENE GRAGG.

Child of HOWARD EFFLER and DEBRA GRAGG is:
128. i. JENNIFER LYNN$_6$ EFFLER, b. February 25, 1976.

Child of HOWARD EDWARD EFFLER is:
    ii. JAKE RYAN$_6$ DAVIS.

79. RICARDO EUGENE (RICKEY)$_5$ BLANKENSHIP (*THELMA MARIE$_4$ EFFLER, SAMUEL OLIVER$_3$, ALFRED ERWIN$_2$, STEPHEN G.$_1$*) was born November 08, 1960, and died December 04, 1982. He married TERESA WHELLER.

Child of RICARDO BLANKENSHIP and TERESA WHELLER is:
    i. MICHAEL JOHN$_6$ WHELLER, b. March 16, 1979.

80. PAMELA ANNETTE$_5$ ROBERSON (*RUBY JOE$_4$ EFFLER, SAMUEL OLIVER$_3$, ALFRED ERWIN$_2$, STEPHEN G.$_1$*) was born June 19, 1963. She married DAVID DENENT STAFFORD.

Children of PAMELA ROBERSON and DAVID STAFFORD are:
    i. TERA MICHELLE$_6$ STAFFORD, b. August 13, 1986.
    ii. BETHANY MARIE STAFFORD, b. November 27, 1989.

81. JAMES BRIAN₅ ROBERSON *(RUBY JOE₄ EFFLER, SAMUEL OLIVER₃, ALFRED ERWIN₂, STEPHEN G.₁)* was born November 09, 1969. He married (1) CHRISSIE LYN CHAVIS. He met (2) CONNIE CLONIGER MILLS 1995.

Child of JAMES ROBERSON and CHRISSIE CHAVIS is:
    i. ANGELA LOUISE₆ ROBERSON, b. October 19, 1989.

Child of JAMES ROBERSON and CONNIE MILLS is:
    ii. THOMAS JUSTIN₆ ROBERSON, b. June 01, 1996.

82. SAMUEL "BO" EDWARD₅ EFFLER *(EDWARD ROY LEE₄, SAMUEL OLIVER₃, ALFRED ERWIN₂, STEPHEN G.₁)* was born May 21, 1973. He married DAWN RENAE WRIGHT.

Child of SAMUEL EFFLER and DAWN WRIGHT is:
    i. SAMANTHA ELAINE₆ EFFLER, b. August 02, 2001.

83. HOWARD DWAYNE₅ EFFLER *(WILLIAM HOWARD₄, JAMES LEROY₃, ALFRED ERWIN₂, STEPHEN G.₁)* was born November 11, 1961 in Newport News, VA. He married (2) LESLIE DAWN MEREDITH March 20, 1992 in Newport News, VA. She was born March 10, 1970.

Children of HOWARD DWAYNE EFFLER are:
    i. DANA ANN₆ EFFLER, b. May 15, 1987.
    ii. LAUREN LEANN EFFLER, b. August 09, 1988, Hampton, VA.

Children of HOWARD EFFLER and LESLIE MEREDITH are:
    iii. KENDALL DAWN₆ EFFLER, b. November 16, 1994, Newport News, VA.
    iv. MICHAEL LEE EFFLER, b. May 31, 1998, Newport News, VA.

84. DONITA LYNN₅ EFFLER *(DONALD LEE₄, JAMES LEROY₃, ALFRED ERWIN₂, STEPHEN G.₁)* was born January 25, 1975 in Newport News, VA. She married (1) STEVEN HOWARD LYTLE July 05, 1995. She married (2) JEFFREY ELLIOTT PLEMMONS December 23, 2000 in McDowell County, NC. He was born August 03, 1964.

Child of DONITA EFFLER and JEFFREY PLEMMONS is:
    i. BRAEDEN MARIE₆ PLEMMONS, b. September 30, 2002.

85. REGINA LYNN₅ HENSLEY *(DORIS JEAN₄ CARR, MARGARET REBECCA₃ EFFLER, ALFRED ERWIN₂, STEPHEN G.₁)* was born January 31, 1971. She married CARL WELBORN DEAN May 24, 1996. He was born November 21, 1972.

Children of REGINA HENSLEY and CARL DEAN are:
    i. ZOEY GLENN$_6$ DEAN, b. April 06, 1999.
    ii. DARCY LYNN DEAN, b. April 06, 1999.

86. MICHAEL EDWARD$_5$ CARR *(TOMMY EDWARD$_4$, MARGARET REBECCA$_3$ EFFLER, ALFRED ERWIN$_2$, STEPHEN G.$_1$)* was born February 07, 1964.

Child of MICHAEL EDWARD CARR is:
129. i. MATTHEW$_6$ CARR.

87. TONY LEE$_5$ LAWSON *(RENA MAE$_4$ CARR, IOLA ELIZABETH$_3$ EFFLER, ALFRED ERWIN$_2$, STEPHEN G.$_1$)* was born November 29, 1957. He married SANDRA GAIL CABLE. She was born June 12, 1960.

Child of TONY LAWSON and SANDRA CABLE is:
    i. BRANDY GAIL$_6$ LAWSON, b. February 05, 1982.

88. VICKI RENEE$_5$ LAWSON *(RENA MAE$_4$ CARR, IOLA ELIZABETH$_3$ EFFLER, ALFRED ERWIN$_2$, STEPHEN G.$_1$)* was born August 09, 1959. She married MARK TILSON.

Children of VICKI LAWSON and MARK TILSON are:
    i. TYLER BROOKS$_6$ TILSON, b. August 15, 1982.
130. ii. SARAH ELIZABETH TILSON, b. January 17, 1987.

89. WILLIAM SCOTT$_5$ LAWSON *(RENA MAE$_4$ CARR, IOLA ELIZABETH$_3$ EFFLER, ALFRED ERWIN$_2$, STEPHEN G.$_1$)* was born October 10, 1962. He married BECKY BAKER. She was born August 31, 1962.

Children of WILLIAM LAWSON and BECKY BAKER are:
    i. JASON SCOTT$_6$ LAWSON, b. July 29, 1981.
    ii. ROBERT CHARLES LAWSON, b. June 10, 1983.

90. HARRY RICHARD$_5$ LYTLE *(MARY FRANCIS$_4$ CARR, IOLA ELIZABETH$_3$ EFFLER, ALFRED ERWIN$_2$, STEPHEN G.$_1$)* was born September 22, 1961. He married BARBARA KAY LOGAN. She was born July 30, 1961.

Children of HARRY LYTLE and BARBARA LOGAN are:
    i. KELLIE ANN$_6$ LYTLE, b. April 11, 1985.
    ii. RICHARD CHADWICK LYTLE, b. August 25, 1987.

91. KIMBERLY JEANINE$_5$ LYTLE *(MARY FRANCIS$_4$ CARR, IOLA ELIZABETH$_3$ EFFLER, ALFRED ERWIN$_2$, STEPHEN G.$_1$)* was born September 16, 1963. She married JAMES RANDALL DEAL. He was born September 16, 1963.

Children of KIMBERLY LYTLE and JAMES DEAL are:
    i. KACI JEANINE$_6$ DEAL, b. August 24, 1988.
    ii. KATHERINE BURGIN (KADI) DEAL, b. February 16, 1993.
    iii. ZACHERY LOGAN DEAL, b. May 30, 1996.

92. KEVIN ROBERT$_5$ LYTLE *(MARY FRANCIS$_4$ CARR, IOLA ELIZABETH$_3$ EFFLER, ALFRED ERWIN$_2$, STEPHEN G.$_1$)* was born March 28, 1974. He married BRANDY MACHELE STYLES. She was born October 23, 1977.

Children of KEVIN LYTLE and BRANDY STYLES are:
    i. HUNTER AUSTIN$_6$ LYTLE, b. October 25, 1999.
    ii. JACOB THOMAS LYTLE, b. October 11, 2001.

93. ROBERT DWAYNE$_5$ EFFLER *(ROBERT WAYNE$_4$, WILLIAM LESTER$_3$, ALFRED ERWIN$_2$, STEPHEN G.$_1$)* was born March 16, 1961. He married MARY SCHERER.

Children of ROBERT EFFLER and MARY SCHERER are:
    i. ROBERT AARON$_6$ EFFLER, b. August 31, 1987.
    ii. AMY EFFLER, b. May 30, 1989.

94. LELANA LYNN$_5$ EFFLER *(ROBERT WAYNE$_4$, WILLIAM LESTER$_3$, ALFRED ERWIN$_2$, STEPHEN G.$_1$)* was born September 24, 1962. She married JOHN TRANBERG.

Children of LELANA EFFLER and JOHN TRANBERG are:
    i. DANIELLE$_6$ TRANBERG, b. November 03, 1985.
    ii. KALI TRANBERG, b. February 25, 1987.

95. CHRISTIE JANE$_5$ EFFLER *(ROBERT WAYNE$_4$, WILLIAM LESTER$_3$, ALFRED ERWIN$_2$, STEPHEN G.$_1$)* was born March 08, 1964. She married ANDY BAKER.

Children of CHRISTIE EFFLER and ANDY BAKER are:
    i. DYLAN$_6$ BAKER, b. March 18, 1992.
    ii. STEVE BAKER, b. August 23, 1994.

96. REBECCA LEIGH$_5$ EFFLER *(JOHN LOUIS$_4$, LEWIS EDWARD$_3$, ALFRED ERWIN$_2$, STEPHEN G.$_1$)* She married (1) DONALD MALONE. She married (2) EDMOND FISHER.

Children of REBECCA EFFLER and DONALD MALONE are:
 i. DREW MATTHEW$_6$ MALONE.
 ii. SARAH MAE MALONE.

97. ANGELA GAIL$_5$ EFFLER *(JOHN LOUIS$_4$, LEWIS EDWARD$_3$, ALFRED ERWIN$_2$, STEPHEN G.$_1$)* She married ROGER GLENN BURACKER.

Children of ANGELA EFFLER and ROGER BURACKER are:
 i. ALLISON GAIL$_6$ BURACKER.
 ii. AVA NOEL BURACKER.

98. MICHELLE LORENE$_5$ EFFLER *(ALFRED EUGENE "GENE"$_4$, LEWIS EDWARD$_3$, ALFRED ERWIN$_2$, STEPHEN G.$_1$)* was born May 18, 1970. She married MALE STROUD.

Child of MICHELLE EFFLER and MALE STROUD is:
 i. BROOKE ALLISON$_6$ STROUD, b. December 28, 1989.

99. MATTHEW CHARLES$_5$ EFFLER *(WILLIAM CHARLES$_4$, CALVIN FLOYD$_3$, ALFRED ERWIN$_2$, STEPHEN G.$_1$)* was born October 05, 1978. He married (1) JESSICA NICOLE BUCHANAN November 27, 1998. He married (2) JAMIE Abt. 2001.

Child of MATTHEW EFFLER and JESSICA BUCHANAN is:
 i. ALEXIS MONTGOMERY$_6$ EFFLER, b. September 08, 1998.

Child of MATTHEW EFFLER and JAMIE is:
 ii. MATTHEW GAGE$_6$ EFFLER, b. January 2002.

100. KENNETH$_5$ BAILEY *(AGNES LOUISE$_4$ EFFLER, THOMAS ALVOID$_3$, ALFRED ERWIN$_2$, STEPHEN G.$_1$)* was born February 07, 1970. He married APRIL DAWN PRESNELL. She was born 1972.

Child of KENNETH BAILEY and APRIL PRESNELL is:
 i. LEVI DWAYNE$_6$ BAILEY, b. November 29, 1996.

101. KEVIN$_5$ BAILEY *(AGNES LOUISE$_4$ EFFLER, THOMAS ALVOID$_3$, ALFRED ERWIN$_2$, STEPHEN G.$_1$)* was born July 26, 1973. He married SUSANNE MARIE SUMROW.

Child of KEVIN BAILEY and SUSANNE SUMROW is:
 i. RACHEL MARIE$_6$ BAILEY, b. August 03, 2000.

102. CHRISTINA DE ANN$_5$ BAILEY *(AGNES LOUISE$_4$ EFFLER, THOMAS ALVOID$_3$, ALFRED ERWIN$_2$, STEPHEN G.$_1$)* was born November 10, 1978. She married JASON ALAN METCALF February 14, 1997. He was born March 24, 1978.

Children of CHRISTINA BAILEY and JASON METCALF are:
  i. GARRETT ALAN$_6$ METCALF, b. August 11, 1997.
  ii. BRADLEY FRANKLIN METCALF, b. May 23, 2002.

103. DONNA$_5$ HILL *(JUNE ELIZABETH$_4$ EFFLER, THOMAS ALVOID$_3$, ALFRED ERWIN$_2$, STEPHEN G.$_1$)* was born October 07, 1974. She married GREGORY PYATT August 31, 1996. He was born December 20, 1970.

Child of DONNA HILL and GREGORY PYATT is:
  i. EMMA KATHRYN$_6$ HILL, b. July 24, 1998.

104. MICHELLE LYNN$_5$ EFFLER *(THOMAS EDWARD$_4$, THOMAS ALVOID$_3$, ALFRED ERWIN$_2$, STEPHEN G.$_1$)* was born June 17, 1975. She married MARTY BELTON.

Children of MICHELLE EFFLER and MARTY BELTON are:
  i. CHRISTOPHER REID$_6$ BELTON, b. April 23, 1993.
  ii. BRITANNY LYNN EFFLER, b. May 20, 1994.
  iii. JUSTIN DEWAYNE BOLES, b. December 06, 2003.

105. JAMES WILLIAM (J.W.)$_5$ EFFLER *(THOMAS EDWARD$_4$, THOMAS ALVOID$_3$, ALFRED ERWIN$_2$, STEPHEN G.$_1$)* was born September 22, 1977. He married PAM TEASTER. She was born September 10, 1969.

Children of JAMES EFFLER and PAM TEASTER are:
  i. TYLER EDWARD$_6$ EFFLER, b. May 08, 2001.
  ii. AMBER HOPE EFFLER, b. February 12, 2003.

106. MELISSA ANN$_5$ EFFLER *(THOMAS EDWARD$_4$, THOMAS ALVOID$_3$, ALFRED ERWIN$_2$, STEPHEN G.$_1$)* was born December 01, 1980. She married (1) JOHNNY RAY VINES. She married (2) BENNY JOE LISTER December 23, 1999. He was born October 24, 1978.

Child of MELISSA EFFLER and JOHNNY VINES is:
  i. THOMAS JAMES$_6$ EFFLER, b. October 12, 1998.

Child of MELISSA EFFLER and BENNY LISTER is:
  ii. JOSEPH LEVI$_6$ EFFLER, b. February 21, 2002.

107. RUSTY WILLARD$_5$ LOWERY *(RONALD WILLARD (RONNIE)$_4$, ELVIE GARNET$_3$ EFFLER, ALFRED ERWIN$_2$, STEPHEN G.$_1$)* was born January 29, 1973.

Child of RUSTY WILLARD LOWERY is:
   i. RUSTY JR.$_6$ LOWERY, b. April 29, 1996.

108. TOBY$_5$ LOWERY *(RONALD WILLARD (RONNIE)$_4$, ELVIE GARNET$_3$ EFFLER, ALFRED ERWIN$_2$, STEPHEN G.$_1$)* was born April 07, 1975.

Children of TOBY LOWERY are:
   i. SAMMY$_6$ LOWERY, b. April 15, 1994.
   ii. RANDY LOWERY, b. September 30, 1997.

109. DONALD LEE II$_5$ COLLINS *(SANDRA ANITA$_4$ JUSTICE, THELMA CORALOU$_3$ EFFLER, ALFRED ERWIN$_2$, STEPHEN G.$_1$)* was born January 31, 1971 in Morganton, Burke Co. NC. He married APRIL O'DAY 2000 in Reno, Nevada. She was born May 01, 1971 in Reno, Nevada.

Child of DONALD COLLINS and APRIL O'DAY is:
   i. ELORA LEE$_6$ COLLINS, b. February 14, 2001.

110. TONYA LYNN$_5$ FRANKLIN *(DONNA KAYE$_4$ JUSTICE, THELMA CORALOU$_3$ EFFLER, ALFRED ERWIN$_2$, STEPHEN G.$_1$)* was born September 26, 1970 in Morganton, NC. She married RANDY BROWN May 21, 1991 in Gatlinburg, TN. He was born February 24, 1966 in Lexington, NC.

Child of TONYA FRANKLIN and RANDY BROWN is:
   i. JESSICA LYNN$_6$ BROWN, b. September 09, 1994, Presbyterian Hospital, Charlotte, NC.

Generation No. 6

111. CHRISTOPHER SCOTT$_6$ EFFLER *(MITCHELL EUGENE$_5$, JAMES DANIEL$_4$, GEORGE ADAM$_3$, ALFRED ERWIN$_2$, STEPHEN G.$_1$)* was born May 08, 1973.

Children of CHRISTOPHER SCOTT EFFLER are:
   i. COLLIN SCOTT$_7$ EFFLER, b. May 13, 1997.
   ii. JOEL BRIAN EFFLER.

112. JASON BRIAN$_6$ EFFLER *(MITCHELL EUGENE$_5$, JAMES DANIEL$_4$, GEORGE ADAM$_3$, ALFRED ERWIN$_2$, STEPHEN G.$_1$)* was born August 05, 1974.

Child of JASON BRIAN EFFLER is:
    i. CAITLIN MCKENZIE$_7$ EFFLER, b. April 24, 1994.

113. VERA LYNN$_6$ EFFLER *(DWIGHT MILLARD$_5$, JAMES DANIEL$_4$, GEORGE ADAM$_3$, ALFRED ERWIN$_2$, STEPHEN G.$_1$)* was born July 07, 1977. She married RUSSELL DEAN BRANTON December 06, 1997.

Child of VERA EFFLER and RUSSELL BRANTON is:
    i. RUSSELL DEAN JR.$_7$ BRANTON, b. May 05, 1998.

114. JOSHUA DWIGHT$_6$ EFFLER *(DWIGHT MILLARD$_5$, JAMES DANIEL$_4$, GEORGE ADAM$_3$, ALFRED ERWIN$_2$, STEPHEN G.$_1$)* was born June 11, 1984. He married STEPHANIE LEANNE MCABEE December 05, 2003, daughter of TRAY MCABEE and ROBIN.

Child of JOSHUA EFFLER and STEPHANIE MCABEE is:
    i. BRYSON SAMUEL$_7$ EFFLER, b. November 18, 2002.

115. MALINDA LEIGH$_6$ EFFLER *(ROBERT (BOBBY) MARSHALL$_5$, JAMES DANIEL$_4$, GEORGE ADAM$_3$, ALFRED ERWIN$_2$, STEPHEN G.$_1$)* was born February 18, 1977. She married MALE SMITH.

Child of MALINDA EFFLER and MALE SMITH is:
    i. KALA BROOKE$_7$ SMITH, b. January 23, 2000.

116. DAVID LANE$_6$ DAVIS *(MERRILL LANE$_5$, FRANCIS EARLY$_4$ EFFLER, GEORGE ADAM$_3$, ALFRED ERWIN$_2$, STEPHEN G.$_1$)* was born September 07, 1974. He married MANDY RIPPY.

Child of DAVID DAVIS and MANDY RIPPY is:
    i. TAYLOR BROOKE$_7$ DAVIS, b. August 10, 2001.

117. GARY LEE$_6$ GODFREY *(GLENDA RENA$_5$ DAVIS, FRANCIS EARLY$_4$ EFFLER, GEORGE ADAM$_3$, ALFRED ERWIN$_2$, STEPHEN G.$_1$)* was born March 15, 1972. He married DONNA.

Child of GARY GODFREY and DONNA is:
    i. SAVANNAH MARIA$_7$ GODFREY, b. October 18, 1995.

118. MICHAEL LANE$_6$ GODFREY *(GLENDA RENA$_5$ DAVIS, FRANCIS EARLY$_4$ EFFLER, GEORGE ADAM$_3$, ALFRED ERWIN$_2$, STEPHEN G.$_1$)* was born December 28, 1973. He married STEPHANIE.

Children of MICHAEL GODFREY and STEPHANIE are:
    i. CIERRA RENA$_7$ GODFREY, b. August 12, 1995.
    ii. LEVI MICHAEL GODFREY, b. June 03, 1999.

119. KIMBERLY LYNETTE$_6$ GODFREY *(GLENDA RENA$_5$ DAVIS, FRANCIS EARLY$_4$ EFFLER, GEORGE ADAM$_3$, ALFRED ERWIN$_2$, STEPHEN G.$_1$)* was born February 26, 1977. She married JOEY HARTWELL.

Children of KIMBERLY GODFREY and JOEY HARTWELL are:
    i. JACOB ANDREW$_7$ HARTWELL, b. August 01, 1995.
    ii. BRITTANY LYNETTE HARTWELL, b. July 31, 1997.

120. MICHELLE RENA$_6$ LUNSFORD *(MARTHA CAROL$_5$ DAVIS, FRANCIS EARLY$_4$ EFFLER, GEORGE ADAM$_3$, ALFRED ERWIN$_2$, STEPHEN G.$_1$)* was born September 13, 1972. She married RICK INGLE.

Children of MICHELLE LUNSFORD and RICK INGLE are:
    i. CECILY RENA$_7$ INGLE, b. May 07, 1993.
    ii. BRISTON WAYNE INGLE, b. July 14, 1995.

121. MELISSA DAWN$_6$ LUNSFORD *(MARTHA CAROL$_5$ DAVIS, FRANCIS EARLY$_4$ EFFLER, GEORGE ADAM$_3$, ALFRED ERWIN$_2$, STEPHEN G.$_1$)* was born October 30, 1973. She married DENNIS RANEY.

Children of MELISSA LUNSFORD and DENNIS RANEY are:
    i. ASHLEY MASHELLE$_7$ RANEY, b. January 03, 1994.
    ii. MAKALA JEAN RANEY, b. June 21, 1997.
    iii. BRIANNA SHEA RANEY, b. July 16, 2003.

122. CHRISTOPHER CHAD$_6$ LUNSFORD *(MARTHA CAROL$_5$ DAVIS, FRANCIS EARLY$_4$ EFFLER, GEORGE ADAM$_3$, ALFRED ERWIN$_2$, STEPHEN G.$_1$)* was born July 18, 1977.

Child of CHRISTOPHER CHAD LUNSFORD is:
    i. CEVIN LEE$_7$ LUNSFORD, b. October 31, 1999.

123. RANDY KEITH$_6$ HENSLEY *(JUDY REVONDA$_5$ BARTLETT, EVA ANGELINE (ANGIE)$_4$ EFFLER, GEORGE ADAM$_3$, ALFRED ERWIN$_2$, STEPHEN G.$_1$)* was born October 08, 1968. He married SANDY WHITE.

Children of RANDY HENSLEY and SANDY WHITE are:
i. JESSICA LYNN$_7$ DEESE, b. December 14, 1985.
ii. BRUCE WAYNE HENSLEY, b. January 20, 1988.
iii. MEGAN BROOKE HENSLEY, b. September 05, 1993.

124. PAMELA RENA$_6$ HENSLEY *(JUDY REVONDA$_5$ BARTLETT, EVA ANGELINE (ANGIE)$_4$ EFFLER, GEORGE ADAM$_3$, ALFRED ERWIN$_2$, STEPHEN G.$_1$)* was born October 04, 1970.

Children of PAMELA RENA HENSLEY are:
i. AMANDA DAWN$_7$ HENSLEY, b. May 02, 1986.
ii. DIXIE MARIE LAWS, b. July 15, 1987.
iii. HEATHER RENA LAWS, b. January 12, 1989.
iv. CHRISTOPHER SHANE BAILEY, b. June 16, 1995.

125. JENNIFER LEIGH$_6$ MATHIS *(JUDY REVONDA$_5$ BARTLETT, EVA ANGELINE (ANGIE)$_4$ EFFLER, GEORGE ADAM$_3$, ALFRED ERWIN$_2$, STEPHEN G.$_1$)* was born September 09, 1981.

Child of JENNIFER LEIGH MATHIS is:
i. REVONDA NICOLE$_7$ MATHIS, b. April 04, 1996.

126. LEONARD DOUGLAS$_6$ EFFLER *(LEONARD (BUDDY)$_5$, THELMA MARIE$_4$, SAMUEL OLIVER$_3$, ALFRED ERWIN$_2$, STEPHEN G.$_1$)* was born March 08, 1974. He married CARRIE DEE PONDER.

Children of LEONARD EFFLER and CARRIE PONDER are:
i. JESSIE DOUGLAS$_7$ EFFLER, b. August 04, 1992.
ii. LAURA DAYNA EFFLER, b. May 03, 1996.
iii. NOAH DAVID EFFLER, b. November 07, 1998.

127. JASON DANIEL$_6$ EFFLER *(LEONARD (BUDDY)$_5$, THELMA MARIE$_4$, SAMUEL OLIVER$_3$, ALFRED ERWIN$_2$, STEPHEN G.$_1$)* was born November 08, 1978. He married NAN MACNEEL DONALD.

Children of JASON EFFLER and NAN DONALD are:
i. CHASE DAKOTA$_7$ EFFLER, b. March 14, 1997.
ii. SKYLYR MONTANA EFFLER, b. September 20, 1999.

128. JENNIFER LYNN$_6$ EFFLER *(HOWARD EDWARD$_5$, THELMA MARIE$_4$, SAMUEL OLIVER$_3$, ALFRED ERWIN$_2$, STEPHEN G.$_1$)* was born February 25, 1976. She married (1) JARED D. SHARP. She met (2) MALE PONZINI.

Child of JENNIFER EFFLER and JARED SHARP is:
  i. TREY CORRINNE$_7$ SHARP, b. February 28, 1995.

Child of JENNIFER EFFLER and MALE PONZINI is:
  ii. ALLESAND (ALEX) BERLIN$_7$ PONZINI, b. December 09, 1997.

129. MATTHEW$_6$ CARR *(MICHAEL EDWARD$_5$, TOMMY EDWARD$_4$, MARGARET REBECCA$_3$ EFFLER, ALFRED ERWIN$_2$ STEPHEN G.$_1$)* He married MEGAN GOINGS, daughter of KYM GOINGS.

Child of MATTHEW CARR and MEGAN GOINGS is:
  i. RYLEIGH MCKENZIE$_7$ GOINGS, b. August 05, 2004.

130. SARAH ELIZABETH$_6$ TILSON *(VICKI RENEE$_5$ LAWSON, RENA MAE$_4$ CARR, IOLA ELIZABETH$_3$ EFFLER, ALFRED ERWIN$_2$, STEPHEN G.$_1$)* was born January 17, 1987. She met MALE TAYLOR December 2002.

Child of SARAH TILSON and MALE TAYLOR is:
  i. AUSTIN KYLE$_7$ TAYLOR, b. September 18, 2003.

The Untold Story of
Frankie Silver

Lynn Moss Sanders, *Appalachian Journal:* "(Perry Deane Young) provides important historical background to this fascinating story...Young is able to build suspense, even for a story many of his readers may already know...This personal tone is refreshing in a historical study...By personalizing both Frankie Silver's story and his own search for it, Young has given readers an interesting and well-written book about history and the way it is created."

John Ehle, author of *The Land Breakers, The Road, The Journey of August King:* "Most of my life I've heard stories about a pretty mountain lady who was hanged for nothing more serious than murdering her husband. Here...and I can say at last after one and a half centuries—is the true account, thoroughly researched and beautifully presented. It's a high-road journey into this Appalachian mystery.

Wilma Dykeman, author of *The French Broad, The Far Famil:* "Perry Deane Young has taken one of the best-known stories, legends, ballads of the North Carolina Appalachian Mountains and reconstructed Frankie Silver's murder of her husband in December 1831, and her public hanging in July, 1833, as close to the truth as thoughtful research makes possible. His detailed record of that research reveals a model of professional and personal perseverance that adds a new dimension to an old and riveting tragedy.

Al Stewart, *Our State:* "This book is thoroughly researched and clearly written by Young, who says in the preface, "It's high time we allowed for the possibility that Frankie Silver may have been unjustly hanged." One of several books published recently on the Frankie Silver story, this one is likely to stimulate renewed interest in the case among scholars and others.

OUR YOUNG FAMILY

Michael Joslin, *Johnson City Press:* "What began as curiosity as a child about his forebears has culminated in a valuable contribution not only to Youngs everywhere but to anyone interested in the history of the Southern Mountains."

Joy Franklin, *Asheville Citizen-Times:* "A remarkable genealogy that resulted from 45 years finding answers to his questions...But it is much more than a genealogy. It is a book filled with stories and documentation that tell the intensely personal and human side of the history of a region and how it evolved...in many ways, it is superior to a work of fiction. The people are all real and the stories are all the more compelling because of it..., anyone interested in the history of Western North Carolina will find this a wonderful resource."

About the Author

Perry Deane Young is the author of two plays and nine non-fiction books, including a New York Times' bestseller. Born on a farm near Asheville, N.C., Young has written extensively about Appalachian legends and the facts behind them.

978-0-595-36294-3
0-595-36294-X

Printed in the United States
82147LV00004B/373